PRACTICAL
Model Trains

PRACTICAL
Model Trains
Chris Ellis

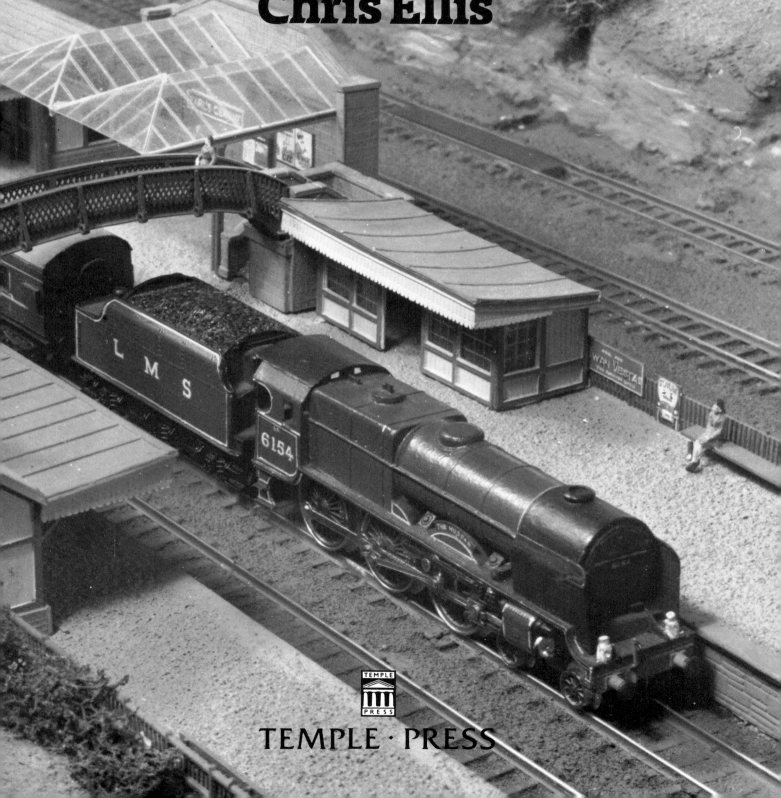

TEMPLE · PRESS

TEMPLE · PRESS

ΠΠΠΠΠΠΠΠΠ

NEWNES·BOOKS

Published by Temple Press
an imprint of Newnes Books
Astronaut House, Feltham, Middlesex, England
and distributed for them by
The Hamlyn Publishing Group Limited
Rushden, Northants, England

First published 1983

ISBN 0 600 34974 8

Printed in Great Britain

Contents

Introduction

Railway modelling is one of the most popular of all hobbies, with an appeal that extends to all age groups and, indeed, to enthusiasts of both sexes. It is easy to see why it is so popular, for real railways are both dramatic and romantic, with plenty of power and action to attract attention. The ambition of many small boys to be engine drivers has been only slightly dampened by the replacement of steam locomotives with diesels and electrics.

Models of railways have been popular for almost as long as real railways have existed, but only mass production on a grand scale during the last 25 years or so has brought the hobby within reach of all, including those with only limited technical knowledge.

In earlier times, model railway enthusiasts had to be craftsmen, because almost everything had to be made from raw materials (what is now called 'scratch-building'). Today one can still choose to make everything from scratch, and there are many who do so. But there are now superb model locomotives, rolling stock, track and accessories of every kind in the larger hobby stores, so that it is possible to construct a layout entirely from manufactured items (called 'ready-to-run' in the hobby).

Most hobbyists steer a course somewhere between the extremes of scratch-building and buying everything ready-to-run, the beauty of model railways being that they have many facets and no definite rules, allowing one to do exactly as one wishes.

I hope this book will serve as a guide for complete beginners, and will also present some straightforward ideas which should be useful even to those who are not new to the hobby but who may be seeking a fresh approach or a new way forward. The author of a book this size cannot hope to cover everything, however, so I have concentrated on the simpler approach to most areas of the hobby rather than explaining the more difficult methods, whose results might look impressive but which are far from easy for the beginner.

What accounts for the appeal of model railways? It might be the movement, for it is one of the few small scale modelling hobbies to offer movement and action, something one does not get with a model soldier, for example. Quite apart from reproducing the fundamentals of real railways by moving trains on tracks, the hobby has the virtue of never being finished. One can always improve by upgrading earlier models as skills increase; scenery can always be rebuilt, layouts altered or extended. If electrics are one's main pleasure, one can get heavily involved in that side of the hobby; those who delight in delicate track work can make their own; those who want to create a three-dimensional landscape can concentrate on scenery. Everyone is better at some things than others, but the model railway hobby is pretty forgiving and will give plenty of pleasure, however good or bad one might be as a modeller!

The main thing is to make a start, to get something running. Do not be afraid to try out the various modelling techniques; skill will quickly follow with experience. Above all, never put off making a start with the old excuse 'if only I had room for a layout'. There is always room for something, if only a diorama, and this book shows some pretty small layouts that will give much satisfaction.

Chris Ellis

Making a start

The beauty of the model railway hobby is that it is infinitely adaptable to suit time, space, money, ideas and imagination. No two modellers do exactly the same thing in exactly the same way. There are no rules.

However, there are some accepted practices and there is a general concensus both among serious modellers and manufacturers to strive for realism within the limitations of personal skill and commercial exedient. Thus virtually all model railway equipment sold today is realistically made and finished, and the very real distinction of only a few years ago – between somewhat crude and simplified 'toy' trains for youngsters and the more accurate and highly detailed 'scale models' for serious enthusiasts – has all but disappeared. Now, with very few exceptions, everything (including the contents of 'starter' train sets) comes into the category of a 'scale model', and it is possible to construct a good-looking model railway layout even if one is a relative newcomer to the hobby. The key to success is making the right choice of model and realising the limitations of one's skills.

Years ago, a great deal – including the track – had to be made from kits of parts or from raw materials, and much skill was necessary for success. Now so many good models are available that it is perfectly possible to buy everything ready-to-run, including the track, locomotives, rolling stock, and all accessories. Even ready-made baseboards can be bought, although most people prefer to make their own. Many also enjoy making some or all their models from kits or from scratch and, again, the choice at any good hobby shop is vast. Most modellers settle for a combination of ready-made equipment and kit building. A typical modeller might buy some ready-to-run locomotives and rolling stock, along with kits or parts to build others. The same modeller might make all the buildings and structures from kits or from scrap materials, and probably most of the scenery too, but these could be combined with scenic backdrops purchased at a hobby shop. The permutations of this personal approach are endless, and one can proceed at one's own pace depending on personal skill, ideas, time available, and, of course, the money in one's pocket! However much mass-produced material is on sale, it can be used in a very individual way.

Do not rush into building a layout without thinking it through first. True, most modellers build several layouts over the years, as more space becomes available, their skill improves, or they have new and better ideas. But many layouts are scrapped on completion because it soon becomes apparent that they have exhausted their potential as far as either building or operating is concerned.

For a complete beginner, it is a good idea almost literally to 'play' trains for a while. Get an oval of track and a few sidings – or use the track from a 'starter' train set – put it on a table top, plug in the power unit and just get used to the idea of running trains, shunting and making up trains, in best 'toy train' fashion. With the modern sectional tracks one can even experiment a little with different track formations. During these early stages read the model magazines, look at plenty of railway books, and get hold of some of the track plan books sold in larger hobby stores.

Starting with a train set The advantage of buying a train set is that it offers a complete package which can be set up right away and trains can be run, if only round an oval of track. Most train sets these days have a power unit, or failing that a battery unit to provide basic power. This might sound a rather childish priority to old hands at model railways, but newcomers of any age want some excitement right away, and getting something running, however simple, often provides the urge to start developing something more ambitious. If the basic set comprises only an oval of track, then one or two turn-outs with enough pieces of track to make up sidings will be sensible extra purchases, making for more interesting operating, even while one thinks more about the sort of layout to build.

Many modellers will naturally think in terms of a layout of their own or one taken from a book or magazine; most serious modellers go in this direction. However, the sort of modeller who wants to collect trains and just needs somewhere to run them should not overlook the work the big manufacturers do to help. Fleischmann, Roco, Märklin, Hornby, Lima (and possibly others) all produce extension track packs which can be added to basic train sets to produce fairly conventional but more complex oval-based layouts of moderate size. Fleischmann offer six stages, Lima three, Märklin four (for K track), and Hornby five stages, each supported by a track pack. They also offer layout books which show how even more complex layouts can be built from either track packs or track components.

Several of these firms also sell what are loosely called 'Toporamas' – mats or coloured printed base sheets which show track layouts and building positions – while the plan books for bigger layouts also give guidance about structure positions and sometimes scenic work. Such a layout will, of course, have a look of 'sameness' about it – rather like a demon-

Above: while it is not necessary to start with a train set, it can be a convenient package. Even this simplest Hornby train set can be used to make a layout with the addition of further purchases and the building of a baseboard

Right: if buying separately it is best to start with a small locomotive, such as this Pemco B & O 'Little Joe'. It is only 4½in (114mm) long but is well detailed and inexpensive, a good starter model for anyone attracted by 'steam age' American railways in HO

stration layout in a shop window. On the other hand, these layouts work well because all wiring and control problems have been sorted out by the manufacturer. For long passenger trains or fast freights, this sort of 'track pack' layout should not be dismissed out of hand. Some of them lack desirable operational niceties like destinations for the traffic, sources of traffic (stations excepted) and so on, but as railway-like settings for running trains they are generally quite acceptable.

The major precaution when buying any train set is to beware of the bogus or simplified models which appear in some of the very cheapest sets – although by no means all of them. Some of the locos are 'junior' items in garish colours, generally non-descript and many are not true scale models. Better, therefore, to go for one of the middle price sets, where the locomotive and rolling stock are accurately finished items from the standard range of an established manufacturer. This means that one's first purchase is not going to be wasted: the loco and rolling stock can be used as the layout grows.

It is best to start with a freight set rather than a passenger set. Beginners have usually not had time to work out which way they will go in the hobby, and very often have no real idea how much room will be available for a layout. By starting with a small shunting or secondary type of locomotive, the investment will not be wasted, because any type of layout can always use the smallest of shunting engines, and on

some very small layouts a little locomotive will suffice until either the layout is expanded or replaced by something more grand.

The 'Alternative' Train Set One can get into the model railway hobby without having to buy a train set to start with. There is a very good case, indeed, for avoiding sets altogether as a beginner and buying exactly what is needed in the way of stock and track to make a start. In this case one can choose a favourite company or type of loco, and buy what amounts to the equivalent of a train set, perhaps making a gentle start with a 'go anywhere' small locomotive that will always find a home on a layout however much it is expanded later.

Rolling stock can be bought in easy stages, say three or four items to start with. Work out how much space is available, what sort of layout and setting to build, and so on, before investing too much money in passenger coaches. As an actual example, long BR Mk I or DB 'Silver Fish' coaches would look quite ridiculous on the smallest type of oval layout: three or more such coaches would take up a large arc of the oval, making it look even smaller than it really is, and they would suffer ugly overhang on the tight curves. An ideal choice for a very small layout would be small four-wheel coaches as made in kit form by Ratio, or the German types made by firms like Roco, Piko, or Fleischmann. A small railbus might be the answer for passenger services . . .

Use of flexible track and readily available kits means that a layout can be started very quickly. This layout uses flexible track and is already operative on bare boards. Card building kits enables structures to be added quickly, even if they are later replaced by scratch-built originals. Here a whole town is being set up. Note the point motor, lower left, which will be concealed by a lineside building. The water tower (extreme left) and platelayer's hut (centre) are already concealing similar point motors

Right: top of the league in miniature railway scales is Gauge 1, 1:32 scale or 10mm to 1ft, on a track gauge of 45mm. One of the latest locomotive models to this size is a Deutsche Bundesbahn Class 212 diesel, with virtually every detail of the original faithfully reproduced externally. Cab doors open and the cab has interior detail

Opposite, top: the size discrepancy between OO and HO is well illustrated by these two British brake vans – OO on left, HO on right – both the same size in real life

Opposite, bottom: there is no reason today why a beginner should not start in Gauge O as there are sufficient kits and models available to make the start. The classic branch line terminus does not take up too much space even in Gauge O if well planned. This station section of Castle Rackrent occupies 16ft (4·88m) of length. It is unusual in being an Irish branch with scratch-built stock but a similar layout could be stocked with ready-to-run models. Note the simple but effective painted backscene and the pleasing style of the structures – also the low platform which always helps a small layout to look bigger. This is the work of R. Chown. Based on the old Waterford and Limerick Railway, it is built in modular sections which make the layout 150ft (45·7m) long on those rare occasions when there is space to bolt all the sections together

Remember that, with a few exceptions, you can mix makes in the same scale. There is no need to restrict rolling stock purchases to one brand name, although one should keep to one area of interest – eg, British, German or American railways.

With a few exceptions, all small scale model railways today are wired for two-rail electrification at 12 volts dc – in other words the running rails also carry and return the current and the locomotive wheels pick up the current from the track. The current is regulated by a power pack – a combination of transformer and controller. Most modern power packs do a good job and all the big model train manufacturers (Hornby, Lima, Fleischmann, etc.) produce very serviceable and reliable units. In addition there are specialist suppliers like H & M, ECM, Troller, MRC and others who offer excellent ranges of more refined power units.

Finally, one must buy the track, preferably a simple oval of sectional track, plus a few extra turn-outs and other pieces, all readily available from any hobby shop. These track items can all be absorbed later into any permanent layout.

Märklin The Märklin system demands a special note because it depends on 16 volt ac control, not the two-rail 12 volt dc which all other systems use. Märklin started back in the days when three-rail, long discontinued by other makers, was the norm. Märklin offered stud contact, however, where the actual centre third rail was replaced by 'studs' which stuck up in the middle of each sleeper. This was an improvement visually on the centre third rail, and a 'skate' below the loco picked up the current. The advantage of the system was (and still is) its electrical simplicity in terms of control and its reliability. Märklin remote control items are particularly easy to fix up and problems of reversed polarity which sometimes arise in two-rail dc (eg in return loops) do not arise with Märklin's ac system. Märklin users

are stuck with its unique system, however, which will not appeal to everyone. Most of their models are German, although some other countries are also covered, all in HO. The original Märklin track is known as M track and is old-fashioned in appearance. Recently K track, which resembles ordinary two-rail track, has been introduced; this is very realistic but more expensive than conventional two-rail track. Peco produce a stud contact strip which can be used with their own Streamline track or, indeed, with other two-rail tracks so that the Märklin system will work on non-Märklin track. One last point to note is that some Märklin locos are produced in two-rail form under the Hamo name.

Choosing the Scale and Train Type Model railways are an international business: models are made for all the big markets – the Americas and the leading European countries – with a good deal of importing and exporting ensuring that models are sold across national boundaries. Thus in both the USA and Britain one can readily buy models of German trains, and similar flexibility exists everywhere to a greater or lesser degree. With so much overseas holiday travel and much in the way of overseas TV and films, more and more enthusiasts are taking an interest in modelling railways of countries other than their own. To some extent, of course, this choice is dictated by limited availability: in Gauge 1, for example, only Märklin offer an extensive range of ready-to-run equipment and they only produce German miniatures; in the USA there are a few models by Kalamazoo, but any British models have to be made from kits or from scratch. Anyone lacking the skill for this has no option but to settle for Märklin and their German types. At the other extreme of size, the tiny Z Gauge offers similar limitations: although some specialist suppliers are producing a few British and American outline models, the bulk of ready-to-run production in this very small gauge is of German types.

About 75 per cent of all modellers go for OO or HO Gauge, this size having established itself over the years as the optimum for most people. Some shops sell nothing but this scale. The trade support for OO/HO ensures a vast choice of sets, models, kits and accessories. The other 25 per cent of the total market covers N Gauge, Z, TT, O, the various narrow gauges and Gauge 1. Of these, N Gauge is widely sold as are the more popular narrow gauge scales (HOe, OO9, On 16·5), but the rest are largely restricted to specialist suppliers – retailers who advertise in the model press.

British Models In Great Britain, OO Gauge is king and the model range is vast, with Mainline, Hornby, Lima, Grafar and Wrenn all providing mass-produced models which are well-known and widely sold. Peco, Wills, Ks, Gem, Ratio, Merit and hundreds of other companies produce a mass of kits and accessories and there are no obstacles to anyone modelling British over a wide area, although late era BR steam and the 'Big Four' private railway companies are the main subjects catered for. Modellers who prefer pre-grouping or the Victorian eras are out on a limb, but not impossibly so for there are ways and means of modelling (and quite a few suitable kits). This wealth of material is available from most British model shops and there are many major mail order suppliers who will serve every need by post. Although one may start off with ready-to-run locos – there are now plenty of good ones – do not overlook the firms like Wills, Gem, Ks and others which make cast loco kits. For relative beginners, there are good 'body line' kits, such as the Wills MR 'Flat Iron' 0-6-4T and the Gem 56XX 0-6-2T which take the Hornby 0-6-0 chassis and fill gaps in the ready-to-run ranges.

A complete beginner is advised to get the cata-

logues and leaflets first, and remember that because of the wide availability of models and the sheer number, OO Gauge is the easiest of all scales and gauges for successful modelling.

British N Gauge is not so rich in choice, but there is more than enough to provide all the average modeller needs. Peco, Hornby-Minitrix, Grafar and

Lima are the big brand names with good ranges, with firms like Gem and Langley (and many smaller) supplying numerous kits and accessories.

British O-Gauge is very limited as far as ready-to-run is concerned, but there are many kit and accessory makers with names like CCW, Chuffs, RTR, ABS, Slaters and Westdale, and several retailers specialise in nothing but O Gauge.

Peco, Gem, and Langley, plus many smaller firms, do a good job between them in supplying the British narrow gauge market with track and kits for locos and rolling stock. For the other minor interest gauges you need to seek out the specialist suppliers.

In both North America and Continental Europe there are specialist importers of British models, mainly in OO Gauge, while in Canada in particular there are quite a number of enthusiasts modelling the British scene. Much the same can be said of other Commonwealth countries.

European Models German models are widely available everywhere in Europe, and names like Roco, Trix, Fleischmann, Lilliput, Lima and Märklin are seen in very many model shops, with a generous selection of locomotives and stock. In fact, it is almost as easy to model Deutsche Bundesbahn in Great Britain today as it is to model the Great Western Railway! Rivarossi offer several German models, while Piko from East Germany offer a wide range and some bargains. Quality is high throughout and it is difficult to buy a German model and be disappointed. There are French, Dutch, Belgium, Scandinavian, Spanish, and Italian models to be bought (the Spanish models are from Electrotren, but the others from the German or Austrian makers listed above). So there is little to stop one modelling a favourite European country. With HO Gauge, of course, the gauge-to-scale ratio is exact so there will be no worries regarding dimensional discrepancies.

N Gauge is superbly well catered for with Arnold, Lima, Fleischmann, Piccolo, Minitrix, Piko, and Roco the names to look for and with models covering Germany (extensively), France, Italy, Belgium, Netherlands, Scadinavia, and Eastern Europe all freely available. Ibertren produce Spanish models in this scale.

Bemo covers HOe and HOm narrow gauge with a big range of German/Swiss models. Lilliput and Roco cover HOe with German/Austrian models. Märklin cover HO, Z and Gauge 1. LGB offer the larger size of narrow gauge as do Faller (in SM32) with the E-train range.

In Gauge O Rivarossi and Lima offer ready-to-run models of a high order, while Rail-Modell and others offer kits. There are specialist firms such as Ade, Spring and Fulgurex offering more highly priced limited run models of European trains on various scales.

American Models There is no problem about supply for the modeller who wants to try American or Canadian modelling. There are specialist retailers in Great Britain and Continental Europe and they invariably offer a mail order service through adverts in the model railway magazines. With American prototype in HO the selection is truly vast and overall prices are probably the lowest of all among models in the HO/OO category. Quality in general is very good. Brand names are Bachmann, Tyco, Mantua, Lionel, Life-Like, Model Power, Pemco, Athearn, Roundhouse, Atlas, Rivarossi (AHM in USA) and there are many others. The Jugoslav firm of Mehanotehnika sells its products under that name in UK and Europe, although they may appear under such names as AHM, Model Power and Life-Like in USA. There is a big following for highly priced brass models, but the rock bottom 'budget' level is well catered for by firms like Life-Like and Bachmann. Relatively few models are actually made in USA, but the degree of standardisation and engineering is generally excellent from countries of manufacture, which include Hong Kong, Taiwan and Italy. Of HO model locomotives made in America, those by Athearn have a particularly good reputation for excellence.

American modelling has some advantages which help the modeller – for example auto-couplers in real life, sharp radius track more common in real life, and good 'compensation' of rolling stock because there are no rigid wheelbase vehicles. A choice of 'old time', steam age, or contemporary does not make for problems because of the selection available. Couplings and wheels are standardised and all makes will mix well. There is quite a following for American modelling in Great Britain and Europe, even a big British branch of the National Model Railroad Association, which is *the* influential organisation in American modelling.

There are a few bogus colour schemes on models to mislead the unwary, but there also happens to be a very good choice of company markings sold in transfer form, enabling repaints to be accomplished reasonably easily. Colour schemes in the USA are generally simpler (eg, all black steam locos) than is the case in Great Britain. The modern era is particularly colourful and because there are many companies operating in USA (and Canada) the mix is interesting.

In O Gauge there are models by AHM/Rivarossi, Roco and All-Nation. Narrow gauge is mainly catered for with limited run brass models and kits among them from the firm of Joe Works. N Gauge is widely available, with models by Arnold, Minitrix, Bachmann, Life-Like, Model Power, Atlas, Roundhouse and many others.

Summing Up There are thus no real limits to the choice of railway to model. It could be one of the famous British 'Big Four', it could be modern British Rail, it could be the Wild West, modern USA, US railroads of the 1930s, modern Deutsche Bundesbahn, Spanish or French, or Welsh narrow gauge. It could be a modern 'preserved' line with a mix of museum stock – old and new – such as could be found on the Bluebell Line or one of the other famous tourist lines.

Most will be inspired in a choice of model by personal experiences – there are hundreds of possible directions the modeller can take. The fun comes in using imaginationand skill to turn such ideas into an actual layout.

Finally, in these early days, there is the need to do as much personal research as possible. Apart from the several model railway magazines available – all invaluable as a source of ideas, information, and new product news and reviews – there are hundreds of books available on all aspects of railways. Read them avidly, absorb the information, take notes, and get thoroughly familiar with the subject.

Lack of a large area need not preclude the building of a realistic layout. The Dalcross line by Tony Pierce which is a classic development from a basic OO Gauge train set oval in a space of 5ft × 3ft (1·52m × 0·91m) and is packed with character. It features a run-round loop and a siding, but the centre-piece is the big and prosperous Bleeding Heart Ironworks which the railway serves. There is a station too. Secret of success is the large group of buildings which gives a visual break to the oval nature of the layout, together with the careful and authentic detailing in an early 1920s period setting. A successful version of this layout could be built by adapting or converting structures from kits. By changing the period, say to the 1930s or 1980s it would look different again, so long as the period detail was correct

Scales and gauges

There has never been a time in the history of model railways when there was only one scale. Enthusiasts have always experimented, generally with the aim of more miniaturisation.

The evolution of ever smaller scales and gauges has, however, been beneficial to the hobby as a whole. Aside from allowing the modeller a vast choice, it means that there is a scale available to suit every requirement, space limitation, and pocket. Thus more and more enthusiasts are able to participate in the hobby, which has contributed to its vast growth in the last 20 years or so.

Each scale and gauge has advantages of its own and it will be necessary to look at them one by one and to see how they fit into the overall scheme of things. But first of all, what exactly is meant by the term 'gauge'?

Most real railways are 'standard gauge' – that is, their actual track width is 4ft 8½in, a figure which just happened to be set by pioneers (like the Stephensons) in the early days of railways and which

has been generally adhered to ever since. There are a few 'broad gauge' railway systems (typically 5ft or 5ft 3in) but most world systems are to 4ft 8½in. In the 19th century there was the famous 7ft 'broad gauge' used by Isambard Kingdom Brunel, the engineer who built the Great Western Railway, but by the 1890s this route had been converted to standard gauge to match other British railways. There are also many 'narrow gauge' tracks less than 4ft 8½in wide, but these will be considered later. The main individual scales and gauges for models will now be considered in order of size.

Gauge 1 – 1:32 or 1:30 Scale This is the largest scale generally considered to come within the scope of railway modelling. There are larger gauges, such as 2½, 5, etc., but these are really model engineering scales involving passenger hauling miniature locomotives which are craftsman-built. Gauge 1 dates from the 1890s, when it evolved at a scale of ⅜in to 1ft, giving a track gauge of 1¼in (45mm) and a scale of

Models in the three most popular scales. *Left to right:* N, HO and O. Locomotive is the Fowler 4F by Lima

1:32. More recently, metrication has seen 10mm to
1ft used for the scale, which is actually a ratio of 1:30.
Visually 1:30 and 1:32 are the same for modelling
purposes.

Although Gauge 1 lost commercial support after
the Second World War, in recent years it has en-
joyed a considerable revival, aided by the re-entry to
the market in 1971 of Märklin, who were one of the
original Gauge 1 makers of the 1890s (along with the
now defunct Bing, Carette, and others). Märklin
produce a wide range of Deutsche Bundesbahn
prototypes of the late steam and recent diesel era,
with rolling stock, accessories and track. Prices are
modest when the large size, robustness, fine detail
and scale accuracy of the models are considered.
Power is 16 volt ac, although dc is available as an
alternative. In the USA, Kalamazoo Locomotive
Works produce a small range of ready-to-run
American models, plus a range of kits. A fine range
of wood and plastic rolling stock kits, all of British
types and relatively easy to assemble, is produced by
Tenmille, while the Japanese firm of Aster make an
attractive series of live steam locomotive kits for
screw-assembly. They are ready to steam as soon as
assembled; although prices are well into three
figures, these are reasonable enough for live steam
models so precisely engineered.

A few other specialist firms make parts or castings
for Gauge 1 and in Great Britain the Gauge One
Model Railway Association is a major force which
has done much to keep interest growing in this scale.
For members only the association produces a useful

range of parts at modest prices. With a growing
number of new items each year, Gauge 1 is certainly
well worth consideration if one likes big models with
super detail. A fair amount of space is needed, of
course, but Märklin in particular have done a good
job in making their track geometry much more compact than one might expect, with a track circle based
on 600mm radius.

**Gauge O – 1:43·5 Scale (Great Britain); 1:45
Scale (Europe); 1:48 Scale (USA)** Gauge O
became popular early in the 20th Century as a more
compact alternative to Gauge 1, because even when
the model railway hobby was in its infancy there was
a trend towards scales which took up less space. The
track gauge is 1¼in (32mm) but the linear scales vary
slightly in different countries, although the discrepancy is small. Modellers often refer to Gauge O as
'7mm scale' (UK) or 'quarter scale' (USA). It will
be seen that the 1:48 scale (¼in to 1ft) used in the
USA is the furthest out as far as track gauge is
concerned for the track scales as 5ft rather than the
actual 4ft 8½in. However, since American stock is to
such a generous size the over-scale nature of the
track gauge is not really noticeable (some purists in
USA work to a corrected track gauge of 1·177in,
which is exact for 1:48 scale; the result is called Q
gauge but it is not catered for by the trade).

In Great Britain O Gauge divides into 'coarse'
and 'fine' scale, but these refer to track and wheel
standards only, not to anything else. This affects the
back-to-back wheel measurement and check rails,

Scratch-built models can be
quite unique, like this superb
and fully detailed NER Raven
Atlantic made by Neil Rose of
Manchester MRS. This is
O Gauge, 7mm to 1ft

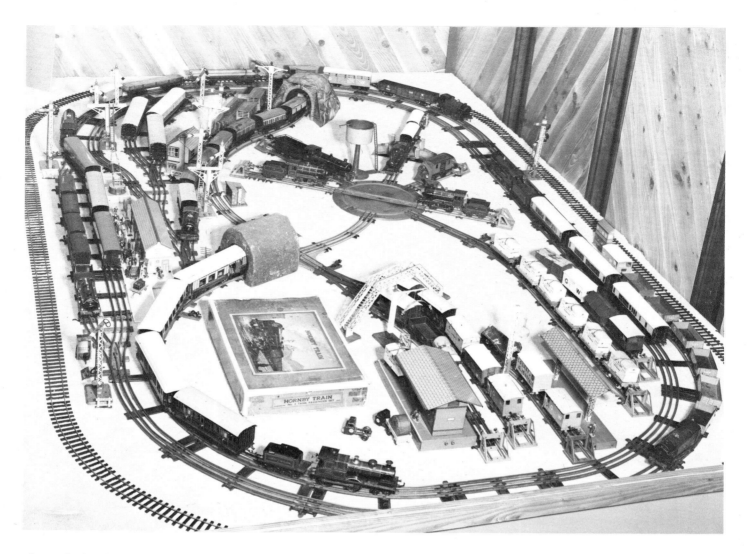

Above: collecting old tinplate models is a specialised part of the model railway hobby. These models of pre-1939 Hornby items are part of the collection of Alan Taylor. Round the outside by contrast is modern sectional O Gauge track by Lima

Right: kits are readily available for narrow gauge models. This 'Cackler' is made from a Peco cast-metal kit for On 16·5. It fits the standard Hornby 0–4–0 chassis which is sold separately

etc. Years ago it made a big difference, but today – with several firms offering ready-to-run equipment – there has developed what is called the 'unified standard', which looks 'fine' in contrast to smaller scales even if it is not 'fine' by definition. Modern O Gauge track, such as that made by Peco and Lima, accepts virtually all current O Gauge models, except those with very deep flanges to the old 'tinplate' standards. A fair amount of ready-to-run material is available: Lima and Rivarossi, both Italian firms, have produced reasonable ranges covering German, Italian, French, American, and British (Lima only) types. All this equipment is to a high standard although it is not so easy to find in the

shops. Certain retailers do specialise in O Gauge, however (and advertise accordingly in the model press).

The golden years of Gauge O were between the wars, when such firms as Bing (Germany), Bassett-Lowke and Hornby (UK) and Lionel and Ives (USA) produced big ranges of ready-to-run Gauge O equipment, all of which is now sought after by collectors. Old 'tinplate' models now command high prices and their collection is now very much part of the hobby in general. The Second World War and post-war austerity brought this big-time O Gauge era to an end as smaller scales took over. However, like Gauge 1, Gauge O refused to disappear and it is still quite possible to model in Gauge O, for there is enough ready-to-run and kit-built equipment to sustain the building of a layout. Track is also readily available. Gauge O is a pleasing scale to work in, perhaps demanding a little more ingenuity than the smaller scales if one is to get the best out of it, simply because the range of locos, power units, and rolling stock is more limited.

Both Gauge 1 and Gauge O share the advantages of size and weight, which give models physical characteristics much closer to those of real railways. Three-link couplers may be used, as in the real thing. Squeaking axle-boxes, the clickety-click as wheels cross rail joins, and the general 'heft' associated with real trains are among the delights of modelling in these larger scales. Prices are often very much higher than in smaller scales, of course, but shrewd perusal of catalogues and adverts will reveal plenty of reasonably priced models.

Gauge S – 1:64 Scale ($\frac{3}{16}$ in to 1ft) This interesting size falls exactly between Gauge O and the popular OO scale. It has virtually no commercial support of any kind in Great Britain, but enjoys rather more in the USA, where locos and stock are available albeit mostly in the form of limited-run brass models at relatively high prices. The US firms of Gilbert and American Flyer used to produce 'tinplate' toy models for Gauge S, which got it started between the wars, but apart from occasional items these have disappeared, although some American Flyer equipment returned to production in 1980. Various kits and accessories are available in the USA, but British S Gauge enthusiasts are few and far between, with a few parts, some – like track – adapted from OO

Gauge from the S Gauge Society. The size is a delightful compromise, however, and some excellent work has been done in this scale. However, one really must be a good scratch-builder to work successfully in S Gauge.

Gauge OO – 1:76 Scale (4mm to 1ft) In Great Britain this is the big commercial scale. There are hundreds of models, sets, accessories, and kits for OO Gauge (also known as 4mm scale) from numerous manufacturers. Probably over 80 per cent of all British modellers work in OO.

The track gauge is 16·5mm, which is a scale of 4ft 1½ in. This is, of course, some way·off the required 4ft 8½ in (which would be 18·83mm in OO Gauge). Just how such a 'narrow' track gauge came about is part of model railway history. Originally the scale was 3·5mm to 1 foot, which is half of the O Gauge. The idea, conceived by enthusiasts in the 1920s, was to produce a compact 'table-top' rail system. Bing produced a tinplate 'table railway' in the early 1920s which stimulated interest, although it was a somewhat toy-like system. It had a $\frac{5}{8}$ in track gauge. The new HO (half O) Gauge was set at 16·5mm track

Above: highly detailed brass models from Japan and Korea are available for HO and O Gauges. This Southern Pacific cab-forward articulated loco was listed at £450 sterling when released in a limited run by Westside in 1980

Bottom: typical of high quality ready-to-run models for British OO Gauge is this well finished and neatly detailed 2300 class 2–6–4T by Hornby

Below: S Gauge at 5mm to 1ft has little commercial support and models must be scratch-built. Cattle truck on right in S Gauge is compared in size with a similar OO (4mm to 1ft) model

Realistic layouts may be made up today by using 'off the shelf' equipment only. Everything in this view, N2 loco and wagons, plus track, is from the Airfix and Mainline ranges, with structures from card kits. Everything is shown as purchased

British models in HO are rare, but the late Jack Nelson worked in this scale (3·5mm to 1ft), specialising in portraying the LNWR, all models being scratch-built. Note here how a simple setting in a cutting captures the atmosphere of 'turn of the century' LNWR to perfection

gauge which is very nearly correct for 4ft 8½ in gauge at a scale of 3·5mm to 1ft.

In the 1920s, enthusiasts in Great Britain postulated an increase in scale for the bodies when it came to reproducing British models. The reason for this was partly because early electric motors were a tight fit inside bodies of British models, and partly because the valve gear and motion (which was necessarily over scale thickness) projected beyond the width of the body when reproduced to 3·5mm scale. The same applied to axle boxes and bogies of rolling stock. The problem was only acute for British models because the loading gauge (permitted overall

dimensions) for British rail vehicles is considerably more restricted than that for American and European vehicles. The idea was taken up, and 4mm scale models running on 16·5mm gauge track became dominant. Hornby-Dublo, introduced in 1938, was one of the main influences. By the end of the Second World War OO Gauge/4mm scale was so firmly established that subsequent attempts to produce commercial models at 3·5mm scale have never been able to make any impression on the market.

It is worth remarking that in the 1930s US OO Gauge was also quite well established at 4mm scale, but with a nearly exact track gauge of 19mm (a scale 4ft 9in). Apart from a few enthusiasts, however, OO in the USA is little followed today, and few components are available commercially. Gauge OO remains, therefore, peculiar to British models and most British enthusiasts use it despite the incorrect track gauge. For those who want a more accurate scale/gauge relationship, the alternatives are outlined below.

EM Gauge 1:76 Scale (4mm to 1ft) The first attempt to make a better scale/gauge relationship for 4mm scale models came soon after the Second World War, when a track gauge of 18mm was adopted by some enthusiasts (EM = eighteen millimetres); it is now standardised at 18·2mm. Early in the history of OO Gauge, a set of standards for 'scale' wheels and track was agreed, as opposed to

the varying standards for wheels, flanges, etc, previously used by different makers of ready-to-run trains. The 'scale' standards gave a reasonable appearance, but did not, of course, overcome the problem of the narrow track gauge. EM does this successfully, although none of the big ready-to-run train makers has yet produced any EM track or trains. However, recent entrants to the ready-to-run field in OO (notably Airfix) have made their models quite easily convertible in that only the wheels and axles need changing for EM running since the models themselves are made with the necessary clearances for 18·2mm gauge wheels. Many other ready-to-run models can be similarly converted, by accident rather than design. The track situation is not quite so straightforward, but one firm (SMP) now offers EM track and turn-outs at reasonable prices, while Ratio make plastic sleeper bases for home construction.

Behind the EM following is the very energetic EM Gauge Society, which makes a great deal of equipment for members (wheels, bogies, etc.) enabling anyone who joins to get going in EM at minimal trouble. It must be stressed, however, that EM is nothing like as simple as staying with OO. But it is now easier than it has ever been, and it is certainly not impossible even for a relative newcomer to convert Mainline or Airfix stock quite easily for EM running. EM, incidentally, is only applicable to British types.

P4 and S4 Gauges – 1:76 Scale (4mm to 1ft) In the quest for even finer scale, P4 was evolved in the 1960s to give true scale profile wheels running on an exact scale 4ft 8½ in track gauge of 18·83mm (EM's 18·2mm gauge scales just over 4ft 6in). The P4 protagonists were seeking perfect scale reduction from full-size so they went back to first principles and made 1:76 scale reductions of everything – wheels, track, and so on. This means very fine tolerances indeed and although quite feasible as a modelling aim, some experience is definitely useful and careful work is required for success. However, many layouts and models have been produced to P4 standards to prove its feasibility and the firm of Studiolith specialise in P4 products such as wheels, makes many items (like couplings) which are useful to all workers in 4mm scale.

S4 is similar to P4, diverging only in the matter of a few practical matters. Both P4 and S4 have their own societies and journals, and anyone wanting to follow up P4 or S4 should write to the societies for literature and details.

For newcomers, the fact that there are several different standards for 4mm scale may be confusing. In summary, 4mm scale running on 16·5mm gauge track is OO, the popular system widely catered for by the trade; EM is a more true gauge-to-scale relationship with 4mm scale models running on 18·2mm gauge track; P4 and S4 are 4mm scale models running on wheels and track to ultra-fine standards on 18·83mm gauge; the rarely encountered American OO Gauge is 4mm scale running on 19mm gauge track. Everything above the chassis is to a common scale, so scenic accessories and other matters are the same whichever standard is adopted.

HO Gauge – 1:87 Scale (3·5mm to 1ft) Compared with the complications of British type models in 4mm scale, HO Gauge is simple. HO was evolved in Britain in the 1920s as exactly half the scale of O Gauge. As O Gauge is 7mm scale, HO is obviously 3·5mm to 1ft – a ratio of 1:87 full-size instead of 1:43·5. The track gauge was settled at 16·5mm which is an almost exact scale reduction of the full-size 4ft 8½ in standard gauge. In Britain several firms started making HO parts for British type models in the late 1920s and 1930s, but to compensate for the small loading gauge of British rail stock, the 4mm scale (OO Gauge) running on the same track gauge was then evolved (as described in the previous section).

This left HO to be adopted by the rest of the world as a standard small scale. It became well established in the USA and Europe during the late 1930s with several firms manufacturing models in both ready-to-run and kit form. HO has progressed steadily since the Second World War and is now the dominant scale in world terms. Some firms originally made their models to a slightly larger scale (1:82 was typical) but now virtually all available models are to true 1:87 scale. The present range of ready-to-run models is vast. Models are available covering US, Canadian, French, German, Italian, Austrian, Swiss, Spanish and East European countries, as well as odd models covering such nations as South Africa and Australia, although it must be stressed that the latter are hard to find and are few and far between.

Manufacturers of HO models include Mantua, Bachmann, Tyco, Pemco, Athearn, Roundhouse (USA), Rivarossi, Lima (Italy), Fleischmann, Trix, Märklin (West Germany), Roco, Lilliput (Austria), Mehanotehnika (Yugoslavia), and Piko (East Germany), but there are others. Most European makers produce models covering nearly all European countries between them. The selection is therefore huge, with something for virtually every requirement covering both the steam age and the modern era. Most models are available in most countries, although sometimes only from specialist importers.

With HO there is no shortage of kits, accessories, train sets or individual models and there are bargains to be had. Problems of scale-to-gauge ratio do not arise, so there is no variation of track gauge as with 4mm scale. There is, however, room for finer standards of wheels and track to make these closer to true scale. In the USA there has been great progress, largely under the influence of the National Model Railroad Association, which has led to wide adoption by almost all makers of a finer wheel – the RP25 type – which has a small flange and a coned tyre section which gives optimum ride on the rails. It is not a true scale wheel – the tread is too wide – but it gives an optical illusion of fine scale. With the RP25 wheel fine scale rail section can be used (Code 70 instead of Code 100). In Europe the RP25 wheel has not yet been adopted, but some makers like Fleischmann and Roco are using a noticeably finer wheel than a few years ago.

Newcomers to the hobby are often confused by the HO and OO scales and the distinctions between them. In brief, HO track is 16·5mm gauge for

models scaled at 3·5mm to 1ft; OO track is also 16·5mm gauge for models scaled at 4mm to 1ft. HO models therefore are about 15 per cent smaller by bulk than OO models. Some accessory items and track itself are often described as HO/OO Gauge – which means they are suitable for either scale.

Anyone who has followed the OO and HO stories so far might ask why people bother with EM and P4/S4 when it might seem simpler to produce British HO models. Indeed, this has been tried in recent years, both Fleischmann and Lima offering certain models, but 4mm scale is so firmly entrenched on the British market that 3·5mm scale has never made the impact necessary for success – despite the production of some excellent HO British models. There are enough new or second-hand models on the market to enable one to model British HO instead of British OO – but anyone doing so will be ploughing a somewhat lonely furrow!

TT Gauge – 1:120 Scale (2·5mm to 1ft/$\frac{1}{10}$in to 1ft) TT started around 1950 when there was a move in USA to produce a more compact system than HO – one which really would fit on to a table top, hence the TT initials. A scale of $\frac{1}{10}$in to 1ft was arrived at, with a track gauge of 12mm. HP and Kemtron were two leading American firms producing models and parts in this scale; in West Germany the firm of Rokal took up the TT idea with a range of models of West German types, with a virtually identical metric scale of 2·5mm to 1ft. Zeuke in East Germany (later reorganised as Berliner-Bahnen) also made an extensive range of East and West German types with others covering Czech, Polish and Hungarian railways. TT has always been a nicely compact scale, capable of virtually all the detail found in HO models. However, the coming of N scale, which became much more popular, led to a big fall-off in TT modelling. Today only Berliner-Bahnen are left as a manufacturer, but their range is excellent, ideal for anyone who wants something more compact than HO but not as small and fiddly as N. Berliner-Bahnen models are, however, restricted to only European types.

TT3 – 1:100 Scale (3mm to 1ft) With TT popular in the USA and Europe, the British firm of Triang (now Hornby) in 1957 started producing a British TT range. Like OO/HO before it, however, it diverged from the existing TT scale for the same reason – the need for larger bodies because of the smaller British loading gauge. The track gauge therefore remained the same, but the linear scale went up to 3mm to 1ft. Many other firms produced kits, locos, and accessories for TT3, but the coming of N scale again led to the decline of TT3 (Triang ceased manufacture in the early 1960s). There is a very active 3mm Scale Society and it is quite possible to model in TT3 even though there is little for the scale in the shops. More constructive work is needed since almost everything must be made from kits or parts. Some 3mm scale modellers work in TM, which uses 14·2mm track gauge to bring the gauge up to correct scale width.

N Gauge – 1:160 Scale (1·9mm to 1ft) There was a long period when some keen modellers investigated the possibility of an ultra-small scale, about half the size of HO or OO. By the late 1920s a few experimental models were made by pioneer enthusiasts, but these were regarded as rather interesting but impractical experiments. It was not until 1960 that Arnold and Trix (as Minitrix) produced working systems with 9mm track gauge. The scale ratio to meet this track gauge was 1:160 giving an actual scale of 1·9mm to 1ft. This is slightly less than half OO Gauge and slightly more than half of HO. N Gauge quickly became the second most popular scale (after HO/OO) and there are many makers, among them Arnold, Minitrix, Fleischmann (West Germany), Piko (East Germany), Bachmann, Model Power, Kadee, Atlas (USA), Roco (Austria), Ibertren (Spain) and Lima and Rivarossi (Italy). Numerous accessory items, structure kits and track units are available and anyone wanting an alternative to OO or HO need look no further than N. By volume, N Gauge is about a quarter the size of OO or HO and therefore a layout can be made in a space where an OO/HO layout would be impossible – or a much more complex layout can be built in a space where only a small OO/HO layout could be housed. All the different makes of N Gauge equipment are compatible in track, wheel and coupling standards – not the case in OO/HO, where wheel profiles and

Opposite: American outline HO is increasingly popular, even outside the USA. This simple short line layout, with characteristic timber trestle bridge, short train, and elderly small tank engine captures the atmosphere of the 1930s in the foothills of the Rockies

Despite being only a few inches long in N scale, this Swiss Crocodile articulated loco by Arnold has every conceivable detail, and is typical of the quality of recent models

Right: a virtue of N Gauge is that it allows quite extensive layouts in a small space. This little GWR line captures the spaciousness of GWR country stations yet forms part of an oval layout smaller than 4ft × 3ft (1·22m × 0·91m)

Opposite, top: very smallest commercial scale is Z Gauge (1:220) and the smallest locomotive made in this scale by Märklin, a DB Class 89, is smaller than a matchbox

Opposite, bottom: 1:32 scale is one of the largest of the narrow gauge scales, using 32mm track. These models are scratch-built, but the figures and accessories are from the Britain's farm series. Models by Vic Hart

couplings differ from maker to maker. Wheel and track standards are on the 'coarse' side, as are the couplers, but everything works well. Most locos are surprisingly reliable despite their tiny size, although some are obviously better than others.

In 1981 Peco produced a finer scale track (Code 50 instead of Code 80) thus making big inroads into defeating the problem of coarse appearance.

British N Gauge – 1:148 Scale (2·06mm to 1ft)
As with TT and HO, British models proved rather too small alongside American and European models, due to their narrowness, so on British models the scale was increased a little on the same track gauge. Thus British models are to a scale ratio of 1:148 instead of 1:160, making them a little over 2mm to 1ft in size. The discrepancy is nothing like as great as it is between HO/OO and TT/TT3. Ready-to-run models are available from Hornby-Minitrex, Grafar and Peco and from Langley and many others in kit form. Although the range available is nothing like as great as the variety of European and American models in 1:160 scale, there is still an excellent selection of models. Peco make track components of special note for N Gauge, but virtually all track and accessories are common to both 1:148 and 1:160 scale. Wheel, track and rail standards are also common.

OOO Gauge – 1:152 Scale (2mm to 1ft Scale)
The pioneers of the 1920s and 1930s were working to half OO gauge for an ultra-miniature scale. They standardised on 2mm to 1ft with a track gauge of 9·5mm, working to very fine standards. This was obviously different from the coarser N Gauge standards used commercially from 1960 onwards by Arnold and other makers. Those who work in 2mm scale OOO Gauge must therefore make virtually all their own track and stock, although a few N Gauge

items and scenic accessories might be adapted. Some exquisite work is done in this scale and there is a flourishing 2mm Scale Society supporting those who choose to work to what amounts to a very fine scale alternative to N Gauge.

Z Gauge – 1:220 Scale (1·5mm to 1ft)
When N and 2mm scales appeared, many people thought that the ultimate in miniaturisation had been achieved. However, the long established pioneer firm of Märklin (West Germany) went pioneering again and produced an even smaller scale – Z – which they also called 'Mini-Club'. This is now a fully fledged system in its own right, making quite feasible a layout on a tea tray or in a desk drawer. Except perhaps for the necessarily large auto-coupler, Z Gauge models make no concession in appearance for their tiny size. They are all excellent little models correctly finished and marked. The smallest locomotives in the range will fit comfortably inside a walnut shell. All models available depict German types both current and steam age. The power is 8 volt dc which means that 12–20 volt rated power units *might* burn out the tiny Märklin motors. Märklin make power units to suit the Z Gauge system, and a few other makes are also suitable. Apart from this, everything is just like the larger scales, the range is big, and there are many accessories on the scenic side from other makers. A British firm have recently produced British bodies to fit the Märklin loco chassis, with rolling stock also appearing, while an American firm have done likewise with an American diesel loco and rolling stock. For the moment, however, the Märklin German range is the one with the most extensive availability.

Narrow Gauges
In addition to the 'standard' gauge scales there are corresponding scales for narrow gauge. 'Narrow gauge' railways are those

with track widths less than the standard 4ft 8½ in. Typically they were built over more difficult terrain or where only light traffic was required. They had the great advantage of requiring less capital expenditure. Certain rail systems, such as those of South Africa and New Zealand, are technically narrow gauge (at 3ft 6in) but these are not normally counted as narrow gauge in modelling terms, for they are run just like standard gauge lines elsewhere, with full size engines, long trains, and all the characteristics of any major rail system.

'Narrow gauge' to the modeller and enthusiast is the world of small engines, short trains, and small railway companies, contrasting greatly with the mainline systems.

Narrow gauge modelling started in the 1950s when several modellers, notably P. D. Hancock, realised that it was possible to reproduce classic narrow gauge style operations by using chassis and mechanisms from one scale, while substituting bodies from a larger scale. Using HO Gauge track with O Gauge bodies, for example, gives a scale track gauge of about 2ft 3in – a favourite real life narrow gauge measure, thus producing a narrow gauge version of O Gauge – in other words, narrow gauge model trains compatible in scale with standard O Gauge models. Narrow gauge trains, however, are invariably smaller than their standard

gauge counterparts and one prime attraction of modelling them is their compactness, allowing a lot of narrow gauge railway to be packed into a small area. Thus it is possible to get a 4mm scale narrow gauge layout into an area of 3ft × 2ft (or even smaller) whereas a standard Gauge OO layout (where the scale of the models is identical) might require 6ft × 4ft.

The main modelling scales and gauges are summarised here.

G Gauge – 1:22·5 Scale (45mm Track Gauge)
The largest scale commonly modelled was introduced by the German firm of LGB during the 1960s. Their LGB (Lehmann Gross Bahn – big train) range uses 45mm track (ie, standard Gauge 1) but the models are built to a nominal 1:22·5 scale. There is some flexibility, with some models of 750mm gauge, others of metre gauge, but all are scaled to fit the 45mm track gauge. The models are 12 volt dc (although some battery powered ones are produced, too) and all are very sturdily made. Although tough enough for children, they are all scale models, superbly detailed and reasonably priced for the size and quality. The srdy brass track is of compact geometry and layouts can be made outdoors or indoors. More recently firms like Merlin have produced live-steam locomotives to this scale, made from quite simple screw-assembly kits, and some structure kits are also available.

SM32 – 32mm Scale (32mm Track Gauge; 16mm to 1ft) This rather loose classification covers all narrow gauge models using 32mm gauge track (ie standard O Gauge). Strictly speaking 32mm scale only applies as a name when the track depicts 2ft gauge types. For types run on 2ft 3in, 2ft 6in, 750mm, or metre gauge, the scale gets progressively smaller, but the term '32mm scale' is used for convenience. Faller E-train, really a toy system for youngsters, offers several models adaptable for the scale, as did the old Triang/Novo 'Big Big Train' system. There are several live steam loco kits available, but most modellers adapt O Gauge chassis and parts. Mamod offer ready-to-run live steam in this scale.

On 16·5 Gauge (7mm to 1ft Scale) This is probably the second most popular narrow gauge scale and is expanding fast. It uses 16·5mm gauge OO/HO track (Peco also produce a special narrow gauge version of it) for trains scaled to 7mm to 1ft. This gives an excellent size of model, as compact as OO Gauge yet with the benefits of the larger O Gauge. All the O Gauge scenic accessories may be used, while many OO/HO locos, wagons, chassis and parts can be adapted; there are also many kits and models on the market specifically to serve the scale.

OO9/HOn2½/HOe (4mm or 3·5mm to 1ft) These are the narrow gauge equivalents of OO and HO standard gauge. The scales are the same (4mm to 1ft for OO9, 3·5mm to 1ft for the others) but the applications are different. OO9 is the British gauge – a scale 2ft 3in gauge; HOe is the European designation for a

scale 750mm. There are many kits and models available, such as a complete range of HOe equipment from Rocko, while some N Gauge locos can be converted. N Gauge loco chassis can also be bought separately to power scratch-built bodies. Of all the narrow gauges, this size is the easiest to start with, due to its availability and compactness.

Ordinary N Gauge track can be used for OO9 or HOe trains, particularly if enough ballast is used to hide the sleepers, which are strictly speaking too closely spaced for 4mm or 3·5mm scale. Peco make a special 9mm Gauge 'Crazy Track', however with sleepers in true narrow gauge style.

HOm (3·5mm to 1ft) Models of the European metre gauge railways run on 12mm gauge. One or two German firms (such as Bemo) make models of German types to this gauge and scale. The track gauge is the same as TT and TT track can be used. A British equivalent is OOn3, using a scale of 4mm to 1ft so that 12mm represents 3ft gauge track – as found in the Isle of Man, for example. Some kits are available for those who wish to model this scale and gauge combination.

HOn3 (3·5mm to 1ft) This is the American equivalent of HOm or OOn3 using 10·5mm gauge track to represent the 3ft gauge lines which were once quite extensive in parts of America. The Denver & Rio Grande Railroad was perhaps the best known of these 3ft lines. Many brass models are produced for locos and rolling stock as are track components and kits, with 10·5mm gauge track from Shinohara.

On3 ($\frac{1}{4}$ in to 1ft) This is the O scale equivalent of HOn3, using 16·5mm gauge (HO) track and providing for the same American types. Models in brass, and many kits, are available.

Nn3 or Nm (2mm to 1ft) The advent of Z Gauge with 6·5mm gauge track has led to the appearance of some kits to enable 3ft (or metre) gauge models to be made, and this is obviously a scale/gauge development which will be taken up more extensively as time goes on.

It will be seen from this that almost any other combination of scale and gauge can be used in narrow gauge modelling to suit individual requirements. For example some modellers have combined TT3 with N gauge to come up with 3ft narrow gauge in 3mm scale, adapting locos and rolling stock to suit, there being no actual kits or models sold for this size. Of all these narrow gauge variations the most popular are On 16·5 and OO9/HOe. There is an energetic and enterprising OO9 Society for those who want to model in this scale.

Overall, as can be seen, the choice of scale and gauge for model railways is rather larger than might at first appear. First choice will probably be one of the popular ones (like OO, HO or N) simply because of the wide availability of equipment. The more exotic one gets in choice of scale and gauge, the more one must be prepared for scratch-building or kit building, as generally speaking there are far fewer available models in the less popular scales.

Where to put your railway

'I'd have a model railway layout if only I had the space' – or words to that effect – are a frequently heard reason for not getting started in the hobby. In years gone by there may have been some truth in this assertion, but with the coming of the smaller scales like N and Z the problem of having space for a layout has largely disappeared. For with these smallest scales a layout can be built on a window ledge.

However, such a layout will necessarily be restricted in scope, for even in N or Z there is a limit to the amount of track which can be fitted on a window ledge. So here is the key to the problem of finding space for a layout. Those modellers who claim to have no space really mean they have no space for the layout of their dreams.

In fact, *everybody* has space for a layout, and the problem boils down to the question of finding a layout or type of model railway operation that fits the space available. No two newcomers to the hobby are going to have quite the same problems when it comes to finding layout space. Even two enthusiasts living side by side in identical small houses are going to face different problems. The houses may be the same, the rooms will be the same size, and even their models may be the same, but one modeller may share his house, while the other may be alone and can choose to use the largest room in the house as a model railway room.

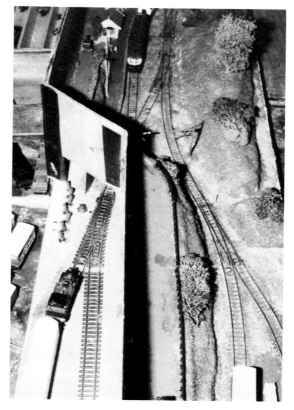

A good view 'behind the scenes' on the simple Thameshead branch showing how the track passes under the dummy road bridge seen in the lower picture and into a fiddle yard which depicts the rest of the line. Note section and turn-out switches neatly set into the board. A completely self-contained small layout like this is ideal for a beginner or anyone short of space

A compact country branch terminus can be built on a 4ft × 1ft (1·22m × 0·30m) board in N scale, as shown here on the Thameshead layout. It rests on the table for operating and is stood on end in a cupboard or slid under the bed when not in use. Note use of commercial backscene pasted on a board. Tray behind holds spare rolling stock. Thameshead is a mythical GWR branch set in Oxfordshire

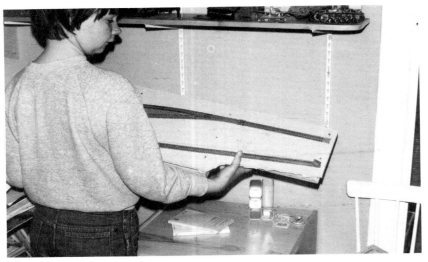

If space is really short a small 4–5ft (1·22–1·52m) shelf with a Z or N Gauge terminus layout will fit on existing spur shelving

the top of a bookcase or a cupboard. So long as there is space for a minimum length of about 3ft or 1m and a width of 9–12in (225–300mm) there is space for a model railway layout. Anything a bit bigger is a definite bonus in restricted surroundings.

These are extremes of the problem – a room freely available or the need to find a minimum space where a layout can be accommodated at a pinch. In between these there are several other possible sites. Most commonly there may be a bedroom or 'den' of sufficient size to allow a shelf-type layout to be fitted around the walls – either on one wall, two walls, or more. Usually this can be a completely permanent layout, although sometimes part of it may need to be portable. There may be an unused hallway or a large walk-in cupboard where a similar type of shelf layout could be accommodated. The space above a stair well or on the first floor landing of a small house has also been used by modellers.

So, before buying, say, the locomotives and stock to reproduce the *Flying Scotsman*, the *Twentieth Century Limited* or the *Rhinegold*, think where such attractive model trains will be run. Unless a layout is very large, big express trains, like these, will look ridiculous. A better approach is to buy a small locomotive and assorted stock to get something running while a realistic layout to build in the space is worked out.

Finding a place to put the layout is the earliest major obstacle, but it is always possible to find somewhere to put a miniature railway, however simple it may have to be. Look for a window ledge, an old-fashioned mantel shelf, the top of a piano, some existing spur-type shelving (for books, etc.),

It is easier to think about portable layouts than it is to build them, for a really good portable layout needs reasonable carpentry skills if it is to be completely reliable. However, folding baseboards are feasible, although a fair amount of care and craftsmanship is vital for success. There is an alternative and that is a single-piece portable baseboard, quite possible with a small scale like N or Z, and not impossible with OO/HO. Such a baseboard might be 3ft × 2ft (0·91m × 0·61m) or 4ft × 2ft (1·20m × 0·60m) as a 'solid top' oval-type layout, or it may be 3ft, 4ft or even 5ft (0·90m, 1·20m, 1·50m) long by up to 1ft (0·30m) wide as a 'module' featuring a self-contained station or yard. In both cases the layouts are light enough to be carried because of

A purpose-built shed in a garden, large enough to hold a 4mm to 1ft scale replica of the area around New Street station, Birmingham, was Don Jones' answer to the space problem. The main line runs round the garden, and this photograph shows the Bull Ring area of Birmingham, complete with the Rotunda. The structures were built from original architects' plans. The figures are actually flat card cut-outs but look most convincing. Part of the main control panel and a 'walk about' controller on a long lead can be seen extreme left

their relatively small size. They may be placed on a table top, across a bed, or on trestles for operating, and they can be hidden out of sight below a bed or sofa or stood on end in a cupboard when not in use. Because there is no folding involved the electrical integrity is not in doubt either. Such layouts can always be turned into permanent ones later if more space becomes available and it is possible (and indeed desirable) to make at least one more section to act as a 'fiddle yard' or second terminus for the main module.

A folding layout hinged against a wall is another possibility for a house where space is at a premium. An area up to 8ft × 4ft (2·44m × 1·22m) can be made either as a 'solid top' or 'open well' baseboard and then hinged to a wall fitting along one long edge. When lowered horizontally the board either rests on existing furniture or on folding legs. When lifted the outer corners are hooked to the wall. This type of layout is quite commonly made but, again, it requires reasonable carpentry skill to be successful. There is a limitation, also, in that unless it is hinged at least 1ft from the wall there will be no room for scenery or structures when the board is in the raised position. This in turn requires framing on the wall to hold the weight of the board, which will be relatively substantial.

Finally there are the more specialised locations. Some enthusiasts, wishing for a domain of their own, have had extensions built on to the house specifically to house a large layout. Others have bought and erected ordinary garden sheds or summer houses, but damp is the enemy of small scale model railways so any such extension or shed needs to be fully insulated on the inner walls or roof. It also needs a proper floor, and a proper electrical fit. If these measures are not taken there will not only be disastrous consequences for the electrics, scenery and structures, as the damp takes effect, but the place will not be very comfortable to work in during the winter months. Conversely it may well be uncomfortably hot in the summer. Much the same remarks apply to garages, even when they *seem* to be warm and damp free.

Again, the loft of a small house is an attractive site for a layout. In a planned loft extension, complete with built in stairway and dormer windows, the structural changes will presumably include insulation and installation of electrics. The alternative of simply buying a portable loft ladder and planking in over the joists is another move which sounds simple. But the inner roof must also be insulated, electric power lines must be run in if they do not already exist, and there may well be beams or roof beams in the way and a restricted working height. So it is not necessarily as easy as it may at first appear.

What is evident is that all the specialised sites, outdoor or indoor, which may seem to offer excellent locations for a big layout, also need considerable capital expenditure and a degree of planning to make them suitable for model railways. Everybody has different ideas and requirements so it can only be said that all the potential problems should be known in advance.

It is worth remarking here that not all the problems of damp and cold will necessarily have such a

disastrous effect on the larger scales such as Gauge O, Gauge 1, or LGB. Many enthusiasts have built layouts in these scales in garden sheds, garages, conservatories, potting sheds, and the like, and they run successfully because the track is bigger, as are the wheels, so electrical contact areas are more generous. But these larger scale layouts are best considered as outdoor lines which just happen to be under cover, rather than as true indoor layouts of the sort mainly considered in this book.

A garden gives plenty of room for a layout in the larger scales and allows gentle curving track just like the real thing. Here is an LMS 'Jinty' with a local goods train on the layout of Don Neale, passing through a rockery

Planning a layout

The big jump from just 'playing trains' to modelling railways comes with the creation of a realistic layout, a miniature environment in which model railway operations take place. Everyone is familiar with the basic idea, for demonstration layouts with scenery are seen in hobby shops and, of course, at the exhibitions which take place wherever there are model enthusiasts. Model railways in a realistic setting really grab the imagination and even non-modellers are usually impressed and intrigued with them.

Train sets, individual locomotives, rolling stock, structures, scenic aids, track, and endless accessories are readily available. Putting all these ingredients together to give a satisfying end result is the secret of success, while the creative skill involved and imaginative use of the models will give personal pleasure and fun. There is a lot of constructive work ahead, but to start with it is necessary to work out the setting for the model railway – the broad canvas which forms the basis for a personal scheme of things.

The key word here is 'personal', for no two modellers will have the same ideas, the same exact preferences, and more critically the same amount of space and time. Therefore no hard and fast rules can be laid down for planning *the* definitive layout, since there is no such thing as a standard procedure. However, key considerations must be taken into account.

There is certainly no shortage of track plans for the modeller to look at. They appear in virtually every issue of the leading model railway magazines, there are specialist track plan books, and the leading makers also offer track plans of their own devising.

Display Layouts Many published track plans are based on the oval format and a great many of those suggested by the big model train manufacturers do little more than utilise the area – say 8ft × 4ft (2·44m × 1·22m) – and pack as much sectional trackage into it as they can. True, there is usually a station, engine shed and freight yard, for example, but nothing goes very far except round the oval. Some of the plans published in books and magazines are like this. Many of the big layouts seen at exhibitions are of this type, even if they are built on a grander scale and are finished with a high degree of realism. If there is the space (really a minimum of 8ft × 4ft in OO/HO) this sort of layout might be suitable for an enthusiast whose main interest is in collecting train models and running them in a realistic railway-like setting. Two typical layouts of this kind are shown here:

Drawing 4.2, based on the actual layout of the Clutch Model Railway Club, is a typical arrangement well suited to club and exhibition use, but ideal also for a family layout if space is available. Storage sidings on one side of the oval can hold a number of complete trains and most of the operation on this sort of layout consists merely of running the trains round the circuit so that viewers on the main station side see a succession of varied trains passing through. Aside from this there is scope for a branch line train to run into a bay platform, some shunting of parcels traffic, and locos working in and out of the loco shed. If a main pleasure is plenty of action with trains of realistic length – named expresses and long freight trains trundling past – then this might be a good layout. It is favoured for club and exhibition use because it has trains moving all the time and allows long runs so that spectators never get bored.

The second plan (drawing 4.2A) is taken from an Airfix GMR plan book and can be made from sectional track. It is much more compact (8ft × 4ft in OO scale, 4ft × 2ft in N), but is better than most sectional track plans in manufacturers' books

Drawing 4.1: a layout based on a station. Bridgnorth on the Severn Valley Railway is a good example of a real station with facilities which make for interesting traffic. This through station could be modelled as one side of an oval layout with what is now the end of the line (at B) extended, or it could be used with a fiddle yard or further sections as an end-to-end wall hugger layout.
(A) Signal cabin;
(B) Carriage sidings;
(C) Station building;
(D) Platform shelter;
(E) Footbridge; (F) Front loco storage road

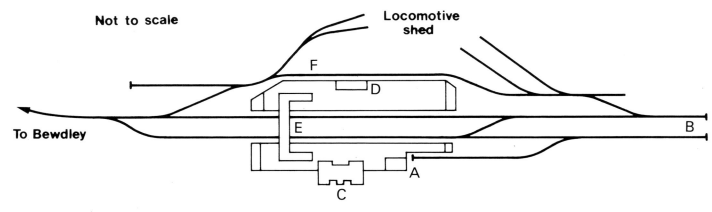

Not to scale   Locomotive shed

To Bewdley

F · D · E · A · C · B

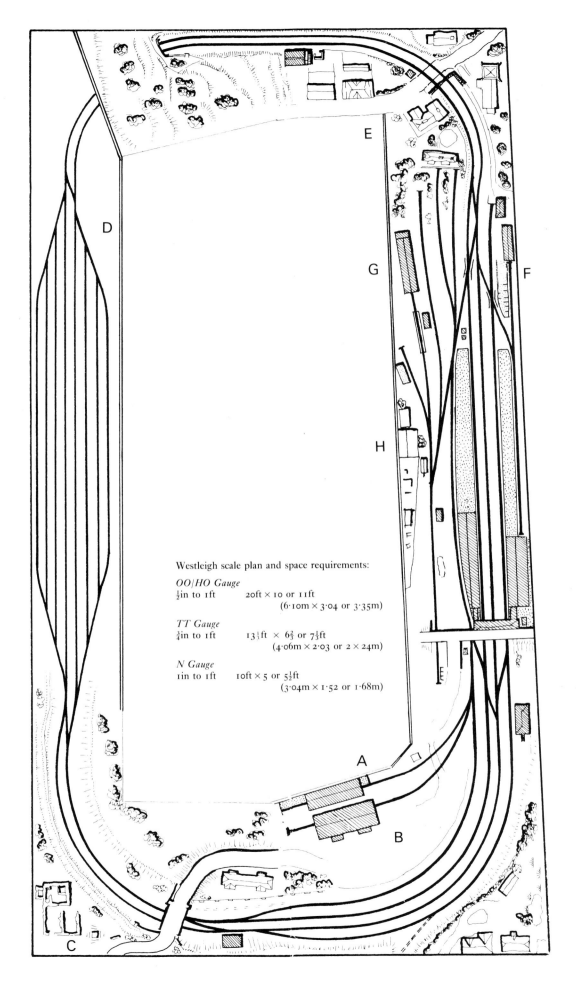

Drawing 4.2: track plan of the club layout of the Clutch Model Railway Club, typical of a large layout with storage roads and a viewing side incorporating a large station area. Note that layout is not exactly square, being wider at the bottom end to take advantage of available space. It could be made in a regular rectangular area, however, by adjusting the trackage at the two ends (drawing by Richard Gardner).
(A) Parcels depot; (B) Goods depot; (C) Ruined abbey; (D) Fiddle yard behind backscene; (E) Little Plumpton; (F) Cattle dock; (G) Loco depot; (H) Timber yard

Westleigh scale plan and space requirements:

OO/HO Gauge
½in to 1ft   20ft × 10 or 11ft
                        (6·10m × 3·04 or 3·35m)

TT Gauge
⅓in to 1ft   13⅓ft × 6⅔ or 7⅓ft
                        (4·06m × 2·03 or 2 × 24m)

N Gauge
1in to 1ft   10ft × 5 or 5½ft
                        (3·04m × 1·52 or 1·68m)

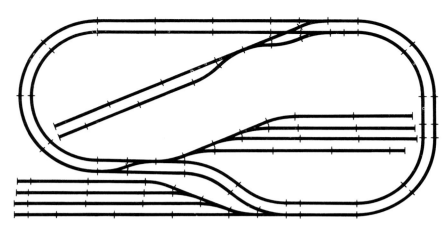

Drawing 4.2A: a typical layout using section track from many suggestions included in manufacturers' catalogues and plan books

because it features two yards and would lend itself well to an industrial setting with the chance to run quite long freight trains. More conventional 8ft × 4ft ovals could be run as country routes, with reasonably short trains such as a 4-4-0 and three coaches as a typical passenger train.

Operational Layouts Now having trains do nothing but go round in circles can become boring after a time for some people. Those whose prime interest is in collecting and building locos and rolling stock may be content just to have a 'cosmetic' setting in which to run them, but for others there is the desire to simulate the actual functions of a real railway. The thrill of highly detailed and handsome locomotive models should not blind one to the fact that real railways are commercial undertakings, however romantic may be the appeal of the trains themselves.

A real railway survives (and with luck prospers) on the revenue it makes from carrying passengers or freight from one place to another – even modern 'preserved steam' lines like the Bluebell Railway earn revenue from the carriage of passengers. If this basic fact of commercial life is taken as a guide, a modeller should not go far wong in selecting (or planning) a layout with good operating potential in which the earning of revenue can be properly simulated in miniature.

On such a layout locomotives will actually be seen to be 'working for a living' with revenue-earning traffic being moved along a route and rolling stock being earmarked for specific loads. There will be sources of revenue on the layout – stations for passengers, freight sheds, industrial concerns, parcels depots, and so on and one can reproduce the essence of real railway operation and serve these various facilities with the appropriate trains. This may all seem very obvious, but a surprising number of newcomers to the hobby do not give this a great deal of thought. As with a real railway there will be a need to work out locomotive rosters, produce operation schedules and keep account of traffic movements. It adds a great extra dimension to the hobby and means that the excitement does not end when layout construction is finished. Choosing a layout with the sort of potential to do all things is an integral part of planning.

A layout with good operating potential does not need to be huge: it can be built in an odd corner, and

the scope it offers for interesting working will more than compensate for the small size. The other point about this question of layout size is that a small layout can be built more quickly, particularly by the less experienced, without the fear of technical complexity, and the smaller the layout the less chance there will be of electrical or mechanical complications. A relative beginner, or an enthusiast short of time, should not feel that it is important to go for a big layout just because there is enough space to fit one in. On the other hand, if there is only a minimal amount of space available, do not despair of ever building an interesting layout.

Getting back to the choice of layout, first of all remember how things happen on a real railway. All the traffic passing along a real line has a revenue-earning purpose, except for track repair or service trains, of course. All the real services are paid for by the users – either as passenger fares or as billings by the railway company to the firms or organisations whose commodities are being carried. If any of these sources of revenue cease, then the railway company suffers as rail traffic is reduced, and in extreme circumstances the entire line closes down because it can no longer pay its way. This is basic economics, but it should be borne in mind for miniature operations as well – a layout should be able to justify its existence in real railway terms by having visible sources of traffic and revenue. The difference between the miniature and real life is that the modeller can control the economics of his chosen area, ensure that model factories do not close down and that passengers patronise the stations – and therefore ensure there is always something for the railway to do.

On a real railway all traffic starts and finishes somewhere. At the various destinations there will be interchanges of traffic in various ways. To reproduce full operations like a real railway would call for a very large and complex layout indeed but to suit individual requirements of time and space only a portion of a line need be modelled and use can be made of the device known as a 'fiddle yard' to depict all the rest of the system. Think of this like a stage or TV play – there is a lot of action in a realistic setting but viewers know that behind the stage set is just a bare area from which characters enter to the visible part of the stage. If a layout is the stage set, the 'fiddle yard' is just one or two tracks 'off stage' from which trains can appear – or trains in the opposite direction head for. Out of your sight (and mind) is whatever the fiddle yard is imaged to depict – a big junction, a city terminus, a major harbour, or just the next station along the line. Or maybe a combination of all these for anything that goes 'off stage' from the visible portion of a layout. This clever compromise helps greatly with the compression and slightly 'make believe' attitude one needs to adopt as imagination is exercised in this miniature world. It helps at an early planning stage to invent even the fiction of an intended layout.

These ideas can now be put together in a very simple layout plan (drawing 4.3) which reproduces all the fundamental requirements for operation in a minimal space. It is the simplest layout in this book, yet it is based on a real railway branch line terminus,

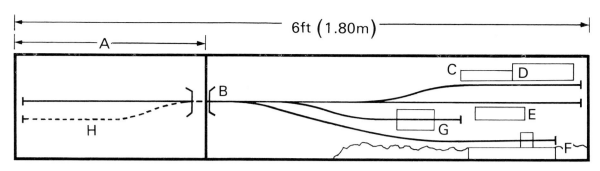

Dyserth in North Wales, and reproduces all its features.

Yes, it *is* simple. For example it is a rare instance in Great Britain of a terminus with no run-around loop to allow locomotives to get from one end of the train to the other. This was overcome by the simple expedient of pushing all freight trains up from the junction, shunting the sidings and running back with the locomotive now leading the train. The junction was 2·5 miles (4km) away at Prestatyn

Drawing 4.3: track plan for a simple layout based on Dyserth station. Scale 1in to 1ft for OO/HO. If space permits extend it longer by 1ft, but 5ft (1·52m) allows the layout to be built in minimum space.
(A) Fiddle yard; (B) Tunnel mouth; (C) Loading bank; (D) Farmers' co-operative; (E) Station building (no platform); (F) Quarry tippler; (G) Goods shed; (H) Optional extra siding

Scratch-building can give eye-catching results. The California Group of modellers made a superb OO Gauge layout reproducing the original Stockton & Darlington Railway of the 1820s, with all stock made by hand

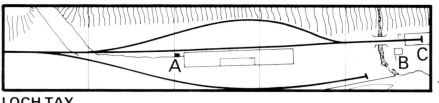

LOCH TAY

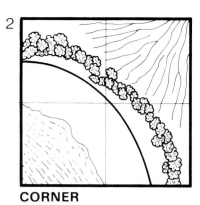

CORNER

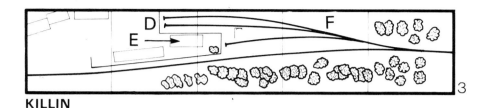

KILLIN

FIDDLE YARD

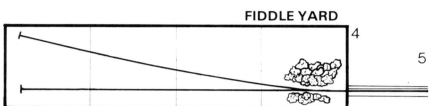

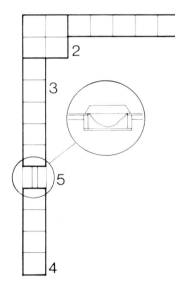

Drawing 4.4: track plan and arrangement of layout modules for a wall hugger in L-shape depicting the Killin and Loch Tay branch. Each square represents 12in for OO/HO, 9in for TT and 6in for N. Inset shows possible bridge arrangement to fiddle yard section.
(A) Ground frame; (B) Small hut; (C) Small loco shed; (D) End loading bank; (E) Goods shed; (F) Scotch derrick

where run-around facilities existed, but Prestatyn and the rest of the railway system is depicted by the fiddle yard area, so this layout merely represents the Dyserth station area. It must be said that this track plan is *based* on Dyserth for it is compressed and the quarry siding is brought parallel to the station road – in real life it ran off at right angles which would take up valuable space if reproduced exactly. For OO or HO the whole lot is got into a length of 6ft (1·80m) on a shelf 18in (457mm) wide (or less, say 15in, 380mm, if the quarry is depicted as a flat cliff face – in other words on a shelf along the wall of a small bedroom it could be compressed even more, to about 5ft (1·5m), if the trains are very short.

So what are the sources of traffic and revenue? Obviously there are passengers and possibly parcels and mail from the station. The station was unusual for Great Britain in having a ground level platform, an enormous visual advantage in a minimum space layout, for built-up platforms make any small space look even smaller. Next there is limestone, the main reason for building the line. The farmers' co-op ships out produce and milk and the loading bank is used for other items like sugar beet. For local goods there is a conventional through freight shed. Thus even this tiny layout has four distinct traffic requirements. A small passenger train (a rail motor or push-pull loco and coach in real life) looks after passenger traffic. Then there would be open wagons and closed vans, and possibly milk vans for the goods and farm produce traffic, and hoppers for the limestone. Even at this early stage one can begin to work out stock requirements – a railcar or push-pull coach with loco, another small loco for freight, at least eight hoppers for the limestone (enough for 'full' and 'empty' trains), at least eight open and closed wagons for the rest, and two brake vans. This simple little layout will keep a solo operator surprisingly busy, yet it only has three turn-outs with an

optional fourth if an extra siding in the fiddle yard is wanted. It is so simple that it can be made up on a table top using sectional track just to try out the potential.

To compensate for the small size there is considerable scope for change. Collect one set of 'steam age' stock, then another of 'diesel age' stock (the branch did not close until 1973), and then as there is no platform one could run a set of American, French or German trains as well, as all would look quite feasible on this versatile little layout. Yet another variation would be to 'bend' the whole track plan to fit a corner or even a bay window if that is the only space you have available. Later this entire layout can be added to a large layout as a self-contained branch in its own right. There are no signals (it operated 'one engine in steam') and all turn-outs were hand-thrown.

Getting on to something only a little more complex, there is the famous Killin branch (drawing 4.4), again closely duplicating a small Scottish branch line.

Originally this branch connected with the Callander and Oban main line at Killin Junction (represented by the fiddle yard) and served the market town of Killin, running on the foreshore of Loch Tay where passengers and freight could (until 1939) take the steamer up the Loch to connect with the Highland main line eventually at Aberfeldy. Again there is a traffic pattern with a single coach train, freight wagons for the pier siding, coal and vans (for market produce) to Killin yard, loco coal for the engine shed, and the little engine shed itself at the end of the line. This branch had a conventional run-around loop and the whole layout needs more space than Dyserth, ideal for a corner of a room. The scrap view shows a suggestion for duplicating a river bridge (which existed in real life) as a scenic link to the fiddle yard section.

These examples show that small branches have much to offer as inspiration for the simpler sort of operational layout. There are scores of other real examples while a modeller can, of course, invent a purely fictional track plan in similar style.

One last example is actually based on an American short line, the Edgmoor and Manetta Railroad which serves industrial customers only in

Left: in its purest form railway modelling reproduces the original exactly. Some years ago the Manchester MRS set out to reproduce the Isle of Man Railway in 4mm scale. Here is Douglas station made in great detail. Track is scale 3ft narrow gauge

Drawing 4.5: layout based on the Edgmoor and Manetta Railroad in compressed form for corner fitting. Each square represents 12in for OO/HO, 9in for TT and 6in for N.

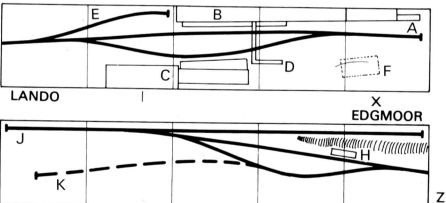

LANDO

EDGMOOR

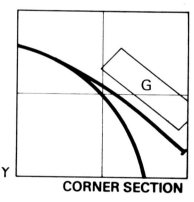

CORNER SECTION

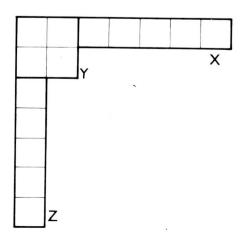

South Carolina using a single o-4-oST tank engine. There was a passenger service once, however. This line connects with blanket mills and the main traffic is box cars which are taken to the interchange with the Seaboard Coast Line. In model form, however, variety could be introduced by providing different industries at the terminus, such as a brewery and a dairy (drawing 4.5).

The small layouts discussed so far are all 'end-to-end' which means that there is very little actual 'mileage' for the trains to run on. Although this is compensated for by the operating potential, many modellers like the idea of the conventional oval-based layout for it is very nice to have the opportunity to run trains endlessly round and round for test and display purposes, or just for the sheer fun of

(A) Boiler house with coal pound; (B) Mill with loading platform; (C) Warehouse with loading bay;
(D) Footbridge over tracks from first floor of mill;
(E) Siding to power station – or some other facility;
(F) Suggested site for depot – passenger station;
(G) Factory; (H) Passenger depot – abandoned on E & M; (J) Track representing Seaboard Coast Line main line; (K) Suggested extra siding for layout – it does not exist on the E & M

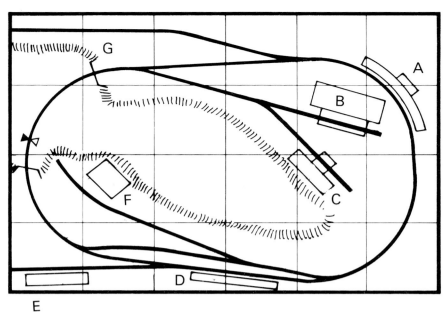

it. One of the simplest examples is the track plan shown in drawing 4.6.

In 6ft × 4ft (1.80m × 1.20m) for OO/HO, or 3ft × 2ft for N, it gives all the ingredients of a fictional branch line with a halt, a station and four sources of commercial traffic (paper mill, distillery, quarry and freight depot as drawn, but these can be varied). All that has happened here really is that a conventional 'end-to-end' line has been bent round and joined up. If it was snipped through at X and straightened it would become something quite like the L-shaped Killin branch.

Examples of continuous style layouts abound in plan books and magazine articles but not all of them offer the traffic and operating possibilities which make them interesting to run. For example, a lot of track plans make no provision for 'escape routes' away from the oval, very useful if one wants to add extra fiddle yards or extend the layout later on.

All the layouts so far shown are for minimum space ideal for solo operators, but if space is available,

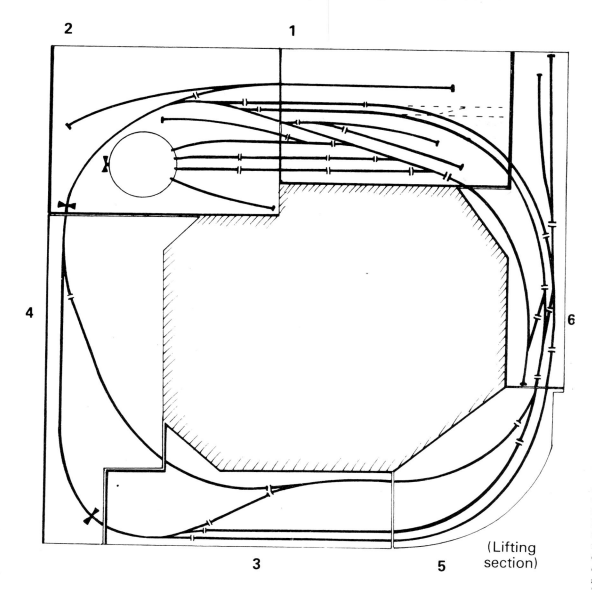

4

6

3   5   (Lifting section)

Drawing 4.6 (*opposite, top*): adapted from the author's Warren Branch (which has the same track plan but different facilities), this is a good basic layout based on the traditional oval. Each square represents 12in for OO/HO, 9in for TT, or 6in for N.
(A) Small halt; (B) Paper or board mill; (C) Distillery; (D) Small station; (E) Goods depot; (F) Quarry with loading tippler; (G) Fiddle yard siding or route to be extended to a larger fiddle yard or any other later extension

Opposite, bottom: another modeller who favours reproducing an actual station layout is Rev Peter Samuels. His layout depicts Bude in the 1930s and the high quality of his work is evident here. Scale is 4mm, EM Gauge. Note the scenic work, with all buildings bedded in, and the very close attention to correct detail in all areas

Drawing 4.7 (*left*): Richard Gardner's Linfield Junction layout occupies a spare bedroom and shows, with adjustments to suit different room areas, what can be allowed for where a complete room is available. The centre is the operating area, the layout boards fitting round the walls of the room. The numbering indicates the order of baseboard development and track feeds and sections. Dotted lines on board 1 depict the original track layout for Linfield terminus

then the sort of large continuous layout, capable of operating in main line fashion, is shown by Richard Gardner's Linfield Junction line in drawing 4.7.

Here there is a main station with a country branch, a loco depot, freight depot, and much else. There is enough 'mileage' to give a 'big time' flavour and passenger trains can be quite long. Most traffic appears as through workings, as do some of the passenger trains, but the layout is big enough to allow display running for exhibitions.

Finally, there is the 'end-to-end and continuous' scheme which really combines the idea of a fiddle yard and terminus with a central section offering a continuous run (drawing 4.8).

The plan shows the author's very small OO/HO Willow Valley line which comprises a 3ft (0.90m) square section with continuous track (a simple oval) from which lead two further boards in an L shape to accommodate a terminus and fiddle yard. Much bigger versions of this general scheme can be found in plan books – the Willow Valley is as small as is physically possible for OO/HO – and in some the two extensions from the oval central section can each be finished as termini sending traffic back and forth. It depends on space.

In summary, time spent thinking about all the track plans is worthwhile. Complexity of track is no indication that any one plan is better than another. The key question is what can trains do once they are on the layout? Sometimes the very simple plans are the best.

Naturally, a first need is to relate a type of layout to the space available, but it is worth repeating that simplicity is a virtue in layout planning. In fact real railways do not make track arrangements complicated where they do not need to. A good example of real life simplicity is seen in Steve Rabone's neat design for Battersby Junction (drawing 4.9).

Here is a modern simplified British Rail station which joins two routes. Trains come in from Whitby and connect with trains for Middlesbrough, while freight trains come into the station and reverse to run off on to the other routes – in other words a Y-shape arrangement. There is a twin fiddle yard in this case, one depicting the Middlesbrough branch and the other the Whitby branch. The entire layout takes 13ft (4m) along one wall with the fiddle yard section taking another 5½ft (1·68m) for OO Gauge (halve these figures for N Gauge). This plan reproduces the exact number of turn-outs of the original

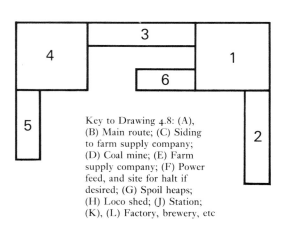

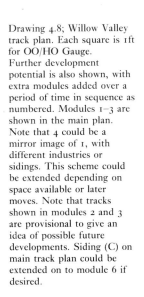

Drawing 4.8; Willow Valley track plan. Each square is 1ft for OO/HO Gauge. Further development potential is also shown, with extra modules added over a period of time in sequence as numbered. Modules 1–3 are shown in the main plan. Note that 4 could be a mirror image of 1, with different industries or sidings. This scheme could be extended depending on space available or later moves. Note that tracks shown in modules 2 and 3 are provisional to give an idea of possible future developments. Siding (C) on main track plan could be extended on to module 6 if desired.

Key to Drawing 4.8: (A), (B) Main route; (C) Siding to farm supply company; (D) Coal mine; (E) Farm supply company; (F) Power feed, and site for halt if desired; (G) Spoil heaps; (H) Loco shed; (J) Station; (K), (L) Factory, brewery, etc

Key to Drawing 4.9:
(A) Whitby fiddle yard; (B) Middlesbrough fiddle yard; (C) Road overbridges with backcloth behind to conceal fiddle yard; (D) Old water tower; (E) Signal box; (F) Tree windbreak; (G) Island platform; (H) Disused platform; (J) Station building; (K) Station Master's house; (L) Barrow crossing; (M) Old line to Picton

Drawing 4.9: Steve Rabone's design which reproduces Battersby Junction as it exists today, with a fiddle yard for each destination. Each vertical division in the station area is 12in apart for OO/HO, 9in apart for TT, or 6in apart for N.

and is not simplified in any way, although it is slightly compressed.

Compression is, in fact, an essential ingredient of layout planning and building. Even a small station like the Ashburton classic would be over 10ft long in OO Gauge, but for model purposes this can be 'selectively compressed' to 5–6ft by making the station platforms and possibly the buildings shorter. In Britain, and some other countries platforms tend to be built up high and they are long enough for the longest trains they handle. To appreciate the size of

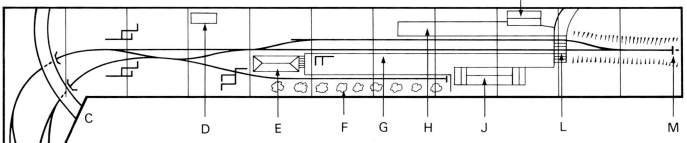

the problem, a suburban station might accommodate twelve coach trains – in OO Gauge terms this would mean platforms 12ft (3·66m) long and a station length, with approaches at least 16ft long (4·88m) which is longer than many rooms in a small house!

Long built-up platforms tend to emphasise the problems when it comes to designing and building layouts. This is why a layout like Dyserth is useful for there is no platform to draw attention to the small area available. For the same reason French, German, American and other types of railway are handy as prototypes since platforms in these countries, except perhaps in big cities, are at rail level with just a cinder or paved area at ground level.

Narrow Gauge The same applies to narrow gauge railways, for these are lightly laid lines which rarely

have elaborate track arrangements in stations and yards. Because the radius is sharp on narrow gauge lines a lot of railway can be got into only about half the area required for a standard gauge layout. Just what can be achieved is shown in the plan for Western Mining Co. (drawing 4.10), a totally imaginary narrow gauge line which serves a mining company – it could be in Canada, America, New Zealand or wherever the modeller wants it to be.

Again, it has provision for fiddle yards or future extensions but the central section is no more than 2ft square for HOe or OO9, or 3½–4ft square for On 16·5 Gauge, so that a modest little layout of this sort could be built in absolutely minimal space. The simple sidings serve the mine and this layout can be fully developed scenically, just like any grander layout. It has an additional bonus in that if the mine structures and scenery is proportioned carefully it

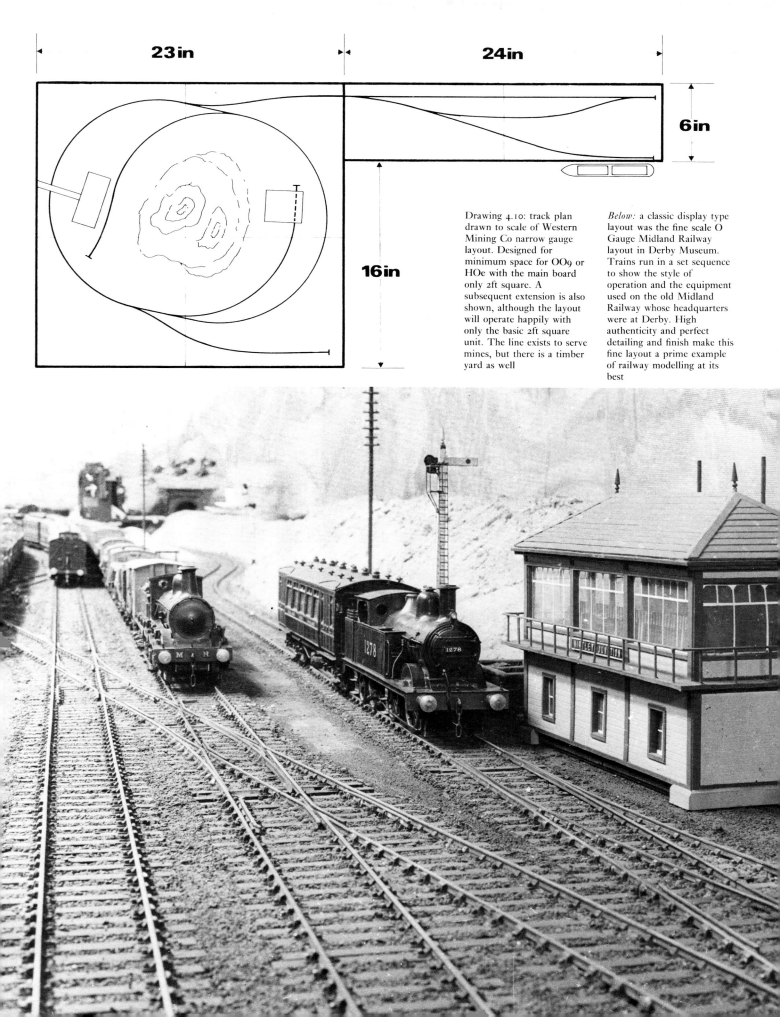

23 in

24 in

6 in

16 in

Drawing 4.10: track plan drawn to scale of Western Mining Co narrow gauge layout. Designed for minimum space for OO9 or HOe with the main board only 2ft square. A subsequent extension is also shown, although the layout will operate happily with only the basic 2ft square unit. The line exists to serve mines, but there is a timber yard as well

Below: a classic display type layout was the fine scale O Gauge Midland Railway layout in Derby Museum. Trains run in a set sequence to show the style of operation and the equipment used on the old Midland Railway whose headquarters were at Derby. High authenticity and perfect detailing and finish make this fine layout a prime example of railway modelling at its best

Above: the Gransmoor Central layout of Manchester MRS shows what can be achieved with N Gauge given good modelling work on the part of the builder. The layout is an oval of the display type with storage roads one side of the oval hidden from view

Right: the use of lining paper to mark out full-size track arrangements can help detect any snags before the actual track laying stage. On Steve Rabone's Z Gauge baseboard the track positions are drawn out and the loop and sidings are being tested for capacity and clearances

can be used for N scale standard gauge operations since the track will of course suit models in either HOe/OO9 or N scale sizes.

Think Modest Most beginners to the hobby have their imaginations fired by seeing big layouts, and it is deceptively easy to picture a vast model railway empire at home with trains running in all directions, spectacular scenery and a fantastic sequence of operations. Obviously, given the time, space, money, and a certain amount of skill, a giant layout can be achieved but it would certainly not be created overnight or even over a period of months. Also bear in mind that many of the very large layouts are very much team efforts, not made by one person but by a syndicate of friends or members of a model railway club.

It is best to start with something quite modest, and if it is possible to expand that initial layout as personal skill increases or additional space becomes available, so much the better.

When it comes to planning a layout, it is largely a matter of working out the available space and then looking for some schemes which will comfortably fit it. Sometimes new modellers sketch out the most dramatic layouts on paper without any great thought of the geometry of the curves, and when the track is purchased it turns out that the visualised track plan will not fit the available space. Here the manufacturer's templates for their respective ranges of track referred to earlier can be invaluable. These aids mean that a project can be drawn out – on ordinary lining paper it is possible to draw out loops, sidings, station throats, and so on, to full-size (some of the templates are actually full-size photographic replicas of the track units). Using these and drawing out the track plan first means that any snags or drawbacks can be seen before a layout is committed. In this manner one should be able to pre-empt any problems before buying track units, so getting exactly what is needed rather than pieces of track which turn out to be unusable.

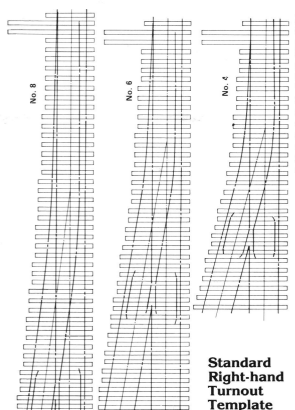

No. 8   No. 6   No. 4

Standard Right-hand Turnout Template

Drawing 4.11: full-size templates in either photographic or drawing form can be used to mark out the track plan full-size before buying all the track. This is the American Boynton version, a much reduced OO/HO sheet being shown here. The turn-outs are cut out for use, but they can also be used as templates for those who make their own track

Various firms make stencils or miniaturised track sections which can be used in layout design. This is the Märklin version

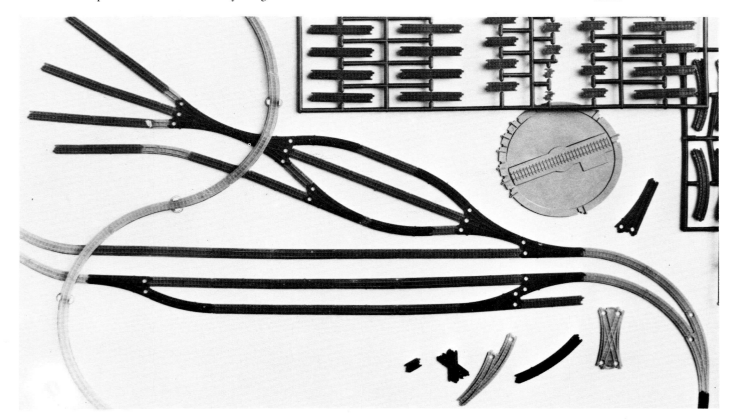

Building a baseboard

Some beginners to the hobby make the assumption that the easiest way to set up a model railway layout is to get a single large sheet of some sort of board, such as plywood or chipboard, and screw the track swiftly into place on top of it. Then they stand it on legs or trestles. This leads to swift disillusionment, for no sooner is this type of board set up than it starts to flex and bow, so the track is distorted and the trains derail. Other beginners sometimes put their layouts straight on to old tables or ping-pong tables. This is slightly better because at least the surface is firm and reasonably well supported. But it is not the answer for a serious model railway layout.

The baseboard is, of course, the essential foundation of a layout and if this is not properly made and

well supported then all subsequent work such as track laying and scenic development may well be wasted effort. If the baseboard is not rigid and well supported to start with then the tracks will flex or distort and no amount of extra fiddling around at that stage is likely to correct the problem.

Grid Framework There are several ways of building baseboards but one of the finest and most reliable methods, tested by time and experience, is the open grid framework. This is made from 2in × 1in (50mm × 25mm) timber of the sort sold by any wood merchant and 'do-it-yourself' shop. This wood is cheap but of sufficient quality for baseboard work and it is easy to cut and join.

In essence the open grid framework consists of longitudinals and crosspieces of approximately 12in (305mm) intervals, the whole making an arrangement of smaller squares when the overall work is finished. This type of construction lends itself equally well to large 'solid' areas such as 4ft × 8ft (1·20m × 2·40m) as it does to long narrow areas like 8ft × 1ft (2·40m × 0·30m). Taking the 8ft × 1ft area as an example, an open grid framework for this baseboard would merely consist of two 8ft long longitudinals with 10in (254mm) long cross-pieces at 12in (0·30m) intervals so that the finished effect in plan view is rather like a ladder. Exactly the same type of arrangement would be used for any other area.

No elaborate knowledge of carpentry is needed with this method of framework construction. One really needs only to be able to draw a straight line, cut a straight line, use a screwdriver and a drill. Assembly is by the conventional basic method of screwing into pre-drilled holes at all the joins. If the work is done carefully and correctly the screws will be the only fixings needed, although most people also reinforce the joins with white PVA woodworkers' glue. This type of framework would be used for a simple layout like Dyserth featured in the last chapter. The cross-pieces can be half-jointed and interlocked in the best tradition of good carpentry. However, with wide sections the cross-pieces can be divided; just screw and glue each piece between the longitudinals.

Obviously, there will be variations in shape and amount of actual construction work depending entirely on the particular layout. Sometimes, for example, the baseboard tapers, requiring extra framing to suit the shape as in drawing 5.1.

Some plans are based in some way on the conventional oval shape and the layout itself may be standing in the centre of a room with access on all

Drawing 5.1 (*below*): variations in open framework grids to suit particular requirements

Drawing 5.2 (*bottom*): joining sections of open framework for larger layouts with operating wells in the centre

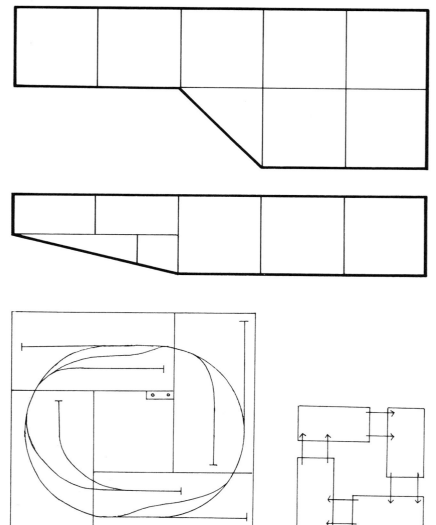

40

sides. Typically a layout of this sort, say, 8ft × 4ft, would be made so that the centre is open for access. It would be usual to place the control position inside this area so that the operator has access to all the tracks surrounding him. The framework for such a baseboard would not be made in one piece, but is best split into four separate parts, each of them made up as a separate gridded section with the appropriate legs or trestles and the four sections are then joined together by screws or coach bolts, in the manner shown in drawing 5.2. This type of framework would be needed for the larger oval type layouts featured in the previous chapter.

Another typical layout shape is the 'L', which might well be arranged along two walls in the corner of a room – a style of board arrangement known as a 'wall hugger'. This layout framework would undoubtedly be made in several separate pieces. The sections would be joined at the corner and along the walls as shown in drawing 4.4 for the Killin and Loch Tay branch in the previous chapter (the Battersby Junction layout, drawing 4.9, would require similar treatment). A small irregular shaped piece

covering the corner section is usually required to give a gentle radius to the curving track it supports.

When selecting a layout thought has to be given to the constructional work needed, and also the actual areas and dimensions of the sort of framework which will be needed for any given baseboard size and shape. Generally speaking it would not be sensible to make any single piece of framework bigger than 6ft × 4ft (1·80m × 1·20m) and even this is a hefty size requiring two people to move it. A convenient length for any given section would be 4–5ft, possibly 6ft at a pinch if the board itself was only about 1ft wide. Keeping in 4–5ft lengths means that any subsequent dismantling and transportation of the baseboard parts will be that much easier. Later alterations will also be easier because a segment of the framing only might be moved from a large layout while that portion was rebuilt. If all the framing is built as one large structure it may well be found subsequently that it cannot be moved to any other part of a building. Also very large single frames may themselves distort or crack due to weight or length.

The beauty of the open framework method of

A delightful scene on John Flann's layout which captures to perfection the atmosphere of a Great Western Railway branch line between the wars

Following pages: N Gauge is well served for German railway equipment. These models by Fleischmann and Arnold are in service on an N Gauge Bavarian country branch modelled by Michael Andress

building baseboards, apart from the lightness of the structure and the relative ease with which it can be built, is the flexibility that comes when one actually puts down the board on which the track will be placed. With an open framework it is not necessary to cover the entire area with one flat board. The opportunity is there to take the landscape below track level by cutting the board which lays over the framing so that gaps are available for features such as lakes, rivers, ponds, gulleys or valleys which fall below track level. It means, also, that one can get away from the flat table effect seen on all too many layouts.

Board Surface The best covering material for the grid is insulation board. Leading brands are Sundeala (UK) and Homasote (USA), although any wood fibre insulation board can be used, $\frac{3}{8}$ in or $\frac{1}{2}$ in (9mm or 12mm) thick. Insulation board usually has to be ordered through a timber supplier and if a layout has irregular shaped boards and sections the timber supplier will normally cut it to suit requirements, provided he is given a sketch and dimen-

sional details. This apart, look in the timber merchant's off-cut bin. Sometimes small areas of board will be on sale cheaply here.

Insulation board is suggested for very practical reasons. First of all the material takes spikes easily when the track is being secured, whereas harder boards require pre-drilled pilot holes, always a difficult and time consuming job on harder woods. It also holds the spikes firmly but not so tightly that they cannot be easily removed. Finally it also makes for quieter running and because it is soft it gives a much better surface for the trains to run on. Avoid such materials as chipboard, blockboard, plywood or hardboard, particularly the latter, because all these materials are heavy and quite often warped due to the nature of their manufacture.

Hence while chipboard and plywood sheeting may well be more readily available than insulation board, do resist the easy temptation to buy these very hard unyielding materials as a substitute. Off-cuts of plywood, chipboard or hardboard may well have their uses as supports for scenery or as formers for back scenes but long experience has shown that

Jim Gadd's neat layout in OO9 recalls the famous Lynton and Barnstaple narrow gauge line on the edge of Dartmoor. It is, in fact, freelance but the style of scenery, stations and stock is close, making the whole set-up very plausible. Setting for the cottage demonstrates a good way to disguise a corner

Opposite: use of ordinary wood planking, treated with preservative, as the baseboard for George Reffin's outdoor Gauge O layout. This useful picture also shows the neat point rodding for lever operation of turn-outs, and the framework supports. Layout operates by stud-contact, hence the studs visible along the centre-line of the tracks

their uses should be restricted to this sort of auxiliary role. Nevertheless, despite all this, there are home modellers who use and swear by chipboard for baseboard surfaces.

There are exceptions to this golden rule about baseboard surfacing. For example chipboard or plywood strips may be practical to carry the road bed on an open-frame grid. For a small transportable or portable layout the ordinary plywood framed door, commonly sold by timber suppliers and 'do-it-yourself' shops is admirable for a small N Gauge layout. The size is most convenient and the price is relatively modest. It is best to cover the surface with insulation board which can be simply glued on to the hardboard or plywood surface of the door or table and clamped in position until the glue sets.

Another exception occurs when considering outdoor layouts. Insulation board is affected very much by water and is quite unsuitable for use outdoors in any circumstances. There are no well defined views on the best materials to use for outdoor layout surfaces, but some enthusiasts have used $\frac{1}{2}$ in marine quality plywood which is resistant to all typical weather conditions provided it is coated with a suitable varnish or wood preservative before the track is laid upon it. It must be emphasised that marine quality plywood should be specified. Ordinary $\frac{1}{2}$ in plywood may look good enough but it is likely to come apart with the ravages of time. Another material which has certainly been used with some success as a surface for outdoor tracks is ordinary soft wood planking of at least $\frac{1}{2}$ in thickness. Most success has been achieved by laying this on to a foundation of breeze blocks and securing it by screws into the blocks. Once again this wood must be most thoroughly treated with creosote or Cuprinol or similar wood preservative before it is set up. Whether ply or wood planking in the manner suggested is used, there is, of course, the problem of inserting the track pins through the sleepers into quite hard and resistant wood. Therefore pilot holes must be drilled out with a bradawl. This is not so difficult as it would be with smaller scales, bearing in mind that most outdoor layouts are Gauge O or Gauge 1; building Gauge OO outdoors simply calls for a good deal more care when piercing the pilot holes in the wood. There is one further precaution which must be taken with respect to wood preservatives. Some brands will react unfavourably with the type of plastic used to make the sleepers of some sectional or flexible tracks. Check carefully for any warning given on the container by the manufacturer regarding corrosive or destructive effects of the preservative. If in doubt cut a sleeper from the track to be laid and coat it with the preservative, leaving it for a few days to see if it has any adverse effects. This rule about using wood instead of insulation board applies to any layout where damp is likely to be experienced. A layout in an uninsulated garage, garden shed or conservatory can also be considered an outdoor layout when it comes to building baseboards, for dampness is always present in such places.

With the 2in × 1in wood framing completed it is a simple matter to place the insulation board over a framework and secure it with screws to the wood at

approximately 12in intervals at the edge and across the transverse framing. It is easiest to screw down through the board into the woodwork, but a perfectionist might prefer to screw upwards through the wood framing and into the insulation board from underneath. The advantage of this is that the surface board complete with track and scenery can be transferred undisturbed onto another framework at some later date. When screwing downwards, there is always the chance that subsequent scenic work or track laying will pass over a screw. Obviously a number of precautions can be taken to obviate this possibility – for example, when the track plan is transferred on to the insulation surface it would be a simple matter to move any screw which is covered by the track and reinsert it further along so that it misses the track bed. In the excitement of building the framework and laying the board such matters as these may seem of no importance, but it is wise to think ahead at all stages of construction.

L-girder Baseboard Construction The standard square-gridded framework with insulation board above it to take the track will satisfy almost all requirements, no matter what the actual shape or area necessary to accommodate the layout. However, it is worth mentioning another useful system known as L Girder Construction which originated in the United States and has been very popular there. Drawing 5.3 shows the principle of the system but essentially it consists of putting the cross-piece above the longitudinal sections, therefore simplifying the carpentry and allowing the width to be varied for irregular shapes, etc. The transverse girders are made in the shape of an inverted L and this gives great strength to the finished structure. There is no need for completely regular spacing of the L-girders, sometimes helpful when there is much spectacular scenery to be made such as ravines and mountains. Indeed, the fact is that space available in typical basements in America allows quite large and spectacular lay-outs to be built displaying extensive scenic work. It is in these circumstances that the L-girder baseboard construction comes very much into its own.

The conventional gridded framework and the L-girder system are not restricted to large flat areas and single levels, and it is not necessary to cover the entire surface of the framework with board. On a shelf-type layout or a wall hugger the track may only require a few inches of width on the overall baseboard, and strips of suitable board, as long as they pass across the framework so that they are properly supported, will be the only necessary flat baseboard surface required. Vertical risers can be put into either the L-girder sections or the square grid and these can be attached as necessary to support the sub-structure for any scenic work such as hills or mountains or the risers can support the track road bed where it is elevated or graded. The framework beneath these mountains can be open, of course, for the surface of the mountains or hills will be carried above the risers and the sub-structure which they support. Obviously, however, a station area or a large yard will still require a large flat sheet of insulation board.

Criss-cross Framing There is a further method of framing which is derived in part from the L-girder system in a simplified form. For want of a better

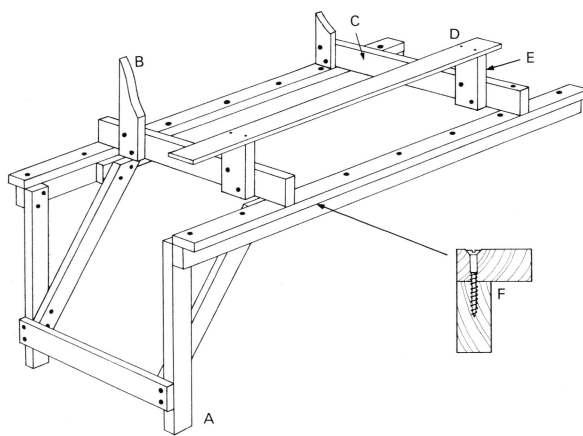

Drawing 5.3: principle of the L-girder construction for baseboard frameworks.
(A) Braced legs; (B) Scenery support as necessary;
(C) Joist; (D) Track-bed;
(E) Risers if required to support track-bed;
(F) L-girder

term, this can be called 'criss-cross framing' because that more or less describes its method of assembly. In this system, instead of fitting the cross-bracing between the longitudinal members, it simply goes across the top.

The dimensional idea of a 12in (300mm) grid is retained as far as possible, but great flexibility is possible in both spacing and dimensions to suit particular requirements. In essence the modular approach is still followed, and the picture sequence shows the assembly of a regular 4ft × 2ft (1·20m × 0·60m) section, a task which took less than one hour including cutting the wood to length.

There are several advantages with criss-cross framing: it is quick; 1in (25mm) square wood can often be used (particularly for N or TT), so it is lighter (and a little cheaper); a mix of wood sizes can be used – say 1in square for the longitudinals and 2in × 1in for the cross-members – as a general rule use larger wood the bigger the module; extra longitudinals and cross-members can be added at will and vary the grid spacing to suit; such pieces can be added retrospectively if more support is required in certain places; one does not have to worry too much about assembling the cross-members in a regular square grid (the cross-members can be put across at an angle if required); if a projecting piece is needed,

just make cross-members longer as required.

These features are shown diagrammatically in drawing 5.4.

Assembly is by glue and screw. It is quickest to screw down from the top since the whole lot can be laid flat and one can literally move along the grid with a power drill putting in the screw holes with great rapidity, or put the screws in from the bottom so that cross-members can be removed or repositioned later on without disturbing the layout. In this respect the approach is the same as for the more elaborate L-girder system.

Putting the screws in from underneath takes a little longer and it requires rather more care to keep the assembly flat, but it can be worth it if later changes are envisaged. The softboard top can also be screwed on from underneath – then it can be moved complete from one frame to another without the need to disturb the track or scenery at all!

Other Considerations Many modellers, when working in smaller areas, find a regular sheet of insulation board very convenient for fixing to the framework, notwithstanding the fact that only the actual track bed area actually needs it – holes can still be cut in the soft insulation board for the building of valleys, lakes, or other features below track

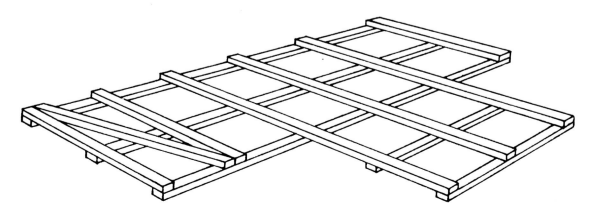

Drawing 5.4: principle of the criss-cross method of baseboard framework

level and sub-structures for the hills and mountains can be built directly onto the flat insulation board surface. There are no specific rules about this and circumstances vary from layout to layout.

There are one or two other points to note with regard to baseboard framing. For example there are other methods of making the framing itself. One very sturdy and fairly simple method is to use handy angle tubing instead of wood battening. The principle is quite similar though, of course the material is different. Dexion girder has also been used by some modellers quite successfully although this needs quite considerable bracing to stop it flexing. A more recent development is the use of plywood cut into strips and interlocked in honeycomb fashion. This gives a very rigid framework although it does require a power saw and a good deal of precision in measurement to ensure that all the pieces interlock. It has the advantage of lightness. A relative beginner is, however, advised to stick by the conventional framework system as described here, although there is no harm looking at these more advanced methods.

After making the framework which is able to take

the actual baseboard surface there is still the problem of supporting it for operation. The most useful way of supporting the gridded framework is to use braced legs. Usually 3in × 1in (76mm × 25mm) or 2in × 2in (50mm × 50mm) battening is used for the main uprights and 2in × 1in or 1in × 1in for the cross-bracing. No elaborate jointing is needed, just two screws at each join. Avoid using glue since it may be necessary to change the leg positions in future and glue would make too permanent a job of the bracing. The actual number of legs will vary with the type of layout and size of the baseboard; for example a very small 4ft × 3ft (1·22m × 0·90m) layout on a gridded framework might just have the braced legs at each end (with the side bracing meeting in the middle) rather in the style of a conventional table. A long wall hugging section, however, will need additional braced legs at 2ft (0·60m) intervals. It is essential to get all legs accurately measured to the same length and to secure them squarely to avoid any tilting or rocking. A spirit level plus a plumb-line and a set square will help to get everything correctly aligned. Wedges may be helpful if one leg turns out to be a shade too short. In the case of a wall hugging layout it is useful to secure the uprights to the wall or the skirting board with an ordinary angle bracket. A typical arrangement is shown in drawing 5.5.

Baseboards for Smaller Scales All the work described so far is required for layouts of OO or HO Gauge or larger; with N Gauge or Z Gauge a much lighter baseboard is practicable. For example a shelf type layout can be made using only 1in × 1in (25mm × 25mm) battening, because there is relatively little weight involved on, say, a 4ft (1·20m) long section. A shelf section for a wall hugger type of layout can be supported exactly like a shelf in these small gauges. Ordinary shelf brackets can be Rawplugged to the wall and are quite sufficient to support the weight of the small locomotives and stock of these smallest gauges. A most convenient idea is to incorporate such a shelf type layout into an

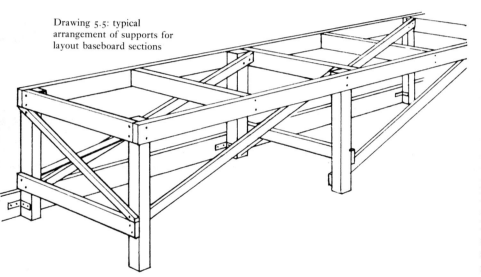

Drawing 5.5: typical arrangement of supports for layout baseboard sections

With the very small scales conventions can be broken. For his small Z Gauge German branch line layout, only 3ft long, Steve Rabone made up an open box-like structure of chipboard which braced itself and had no conventional framing

existing spur shelving system. The spur shelving may already exist to carry books or other objects on the wall.

Other small layouts may also be used without conventional braced legs to support them. For example a small 3ft × 2ft (0·90m × 0·60m) N Gauge layout (which will hold as much track and stock in its scale as a 6ft × 4ft OO layout) may be used without any legs at all. It can simply be placed on the table or across the arms of a chair for an operating session and stood on its end in the corner when not in use. This pre-supposes, of course, that the scenery and structures are either stuck permanently in place or made removable for those periods when the layout is stored out of use. In Z Gauge, some enthusiasts have made complete boxed-in layouts rather in the style of a guitar case, and again these need no separate supports for such a layout can be operated on a table, on an existing shelf, or even across the owner's knee! At this point it is worth again thinking of the scale and size of layout. Clearly there are some attractions in small N Gauge layouts no bigger than 3ft × 2ft for the very reason that they can be put out of sight under a bed or in a cupboard when not in use and the whole problem of supporting the board just does not arise if there is a table or other surface on which it can be placed for operating sessions.

Temporary Folding Supports A layout of the type which folds up against a bedroom wall is also a different case when it comes to supports. One edge for example is supported by the hinge area which would be attached to a projecting shelf and it would

only remain to fit folding legs at the outer corners so that the layout is supported horizontally when it is lowered from its folded position. Hinged folding legs are an alternative to the screwed and braced variety. Some enthusiasts have used these if they are in a profession where they have to move house quite frequently. Instead of being permanently attached to the baseboard framework these legs are made up as a frame hinged below the baseboard framing. A brace may be either separate and screwed in temporarily or it may be hinged to the main legs so that it falls and bolts into place when the legs are in their normal position. Legs of this sort mean that the layout can be taken down in its major sections quite easily for storage or moving.

One last type of support worth considering is the trestle. It is possible to buy painters' trestles of the type used to support planks when painting and decorating, which can also be used to support small layouts of the 6ft × 4ft variety. Some purpose-built trestles of a more substantial type are also available, suitable for this type of layout use. One useful type of support, relatively modest in price, is the folding set of legs produced in metal tubing form to support the cheaper type of small size snooker table. These are ideal for supporting a 6ft × 4ft layout or one of similar area.

Adjacent baseboards present a further problem for if the layout is built in conveniently sized sections as suggested it is clear that these adjacent sections must be joined when the framework for the layout is erected in its permanent site. There are at least three well-proven methods of doing this. The simplest is probably the use of coach bolts through

The use of ordinary folding trestles is a convenient way of supporting small layouts, notably those made in modular form for portability

Using coach bolts to join up adjacent baseboard sections. For photographic purposes the top insulation board covering has been taken off and a scrap of old board below is merely to help show up the bolts. They are normally attached from underneath

holes drilled in the adjacent end faces of the framing. Obviously the line up of the holes through both adjacent end frames is critical and it is usual to hold the framework together with D clamps and drill three or four holes through the two sections so that when the coach bolts are fitted they will align exactly. An extremely popular system of joining adjacent sections, and particularly popular for portable or transportable layouts which have to be frequently dismantled, is the conventional flap hinge. This hinge is used by knocking out the centre pin which pivots the flaps and replacing it with a nail or similar piece of metal of the same diameter as the original pin. When the two hinge halves are interlocked the pin or nail is simply dropped down the centre of the interlocking parts making a rigid and foolproof con-

nection. Separating the adjacent boards is simply a matter of pulling out the pin and separating the two sections. A third method is fairly simple but not so reliable when it comes to lining up sections with great precision. This uses wood dowels and corresponding apertures in the ends of adjacent framework sections. The dowels are simply inserted into the equivalent holes making the whole join fairly rigid (so long as too much weight is not put on the baseboards). It is customary to put a hook and eye across the edges of baseboard sections joined in this manner. The hook is dropped into the eye and resists any tendency for the dowels to be accidentally pulled out of their sockets.

Hard Top Baseboards Despite all the advice given so far in this chapter, there are still many who may already have invested in a chipboard sheet or plywood sheet. It has to be appreciated that such a solid chunk of board will be heavy and may be more difficult when it comes to laying the track.

Such a board has to be braced properly to save the day. For complete beginners drawing 5.7 shows the sort of bracing needed for a 6ft × 4ft or 8ft × 4ft board whether it be plywood or chipboard. Obviously some elementary carpentry is needed to do this, and the use of a power drill speeds up the work, but there is no need for elaborate joints. In general, screw and white glue assembly is all that is required for the framework. The board is then secured by screwing through into the frame.

All this is for those who already have a sheet of plywood or chipboard and want to make the best use of it. A traditional solid top baseboard will still need a framework as shown in drawing 5.6, preferably with insulation board as previously commended.

Having reached the point of a 6ft × 4ft solid top, or boards of similar dimensions, what else has to be thought of? Well, for a start it cannot successfully be put in a corner – and for many people this consideration will rule out this type of layout. If there is one long side and one short side against the corner walls

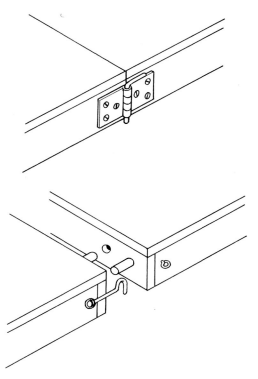

Drawing 5.6: joining adjacent baseboard sections with flap-hinge and pin (*above*) and with wood dowels or pegs (*below*), as an alternative to coach bolts

then access to the far side and far corner is extremely restricted because arms will not be long enough! So the layout will become impossible, or at best awkward to work – this becomes clear the first time the train derails and cannot be reached! Hence if the only site for a OO/HO layout is the corner of a very small bedroom, the idea of a solid top layout may have to be abandoned in favour of a shelf-type or round-the-walls layout.

If space is less of a problem, the best site for a solid top layout is either as an 'island' with access at all edges, or with one short side only against a wall and free access on the other three sides.

The next important matter is the track plan, and this really is important for it can make or mar interest in the layout. Virtually all the manufacturers' catalogues show track formations which fit 6ft × 4ft or 8ft × 4ft areas, but these plans themselves are often too elaborate for the space.

Very often they have loops, figure '8s', even gradients and fly-overs. Surprisingly few of them have the operating potential to match the track, crammed largely it seems on the principle of filling the area with as much trackage as possible. A common feature, for example, is a kick-back spur leading to a turn-table and large engine shed with several roads. It looks good but 6ft × 4ft or 8ft × 4ft is really a very small area in OO/HO terms, even if the board looks enormous on completion, and if there is a large locomotive depot on such a small layout it will be a problem to find duties for all the locos which can be accommodated.

Whether or not it is heretical, less track, not more, is appropriate for a solid top board. Fewer sidings will make the area look bigger than it really is and it is possible to have a really good railway-like system without cramming the board full of track. Tempting as it is to fill all that space in the centre of the oval with big yards and loco sheds, use it instead

for plenty of scenery to break up the oval nature of the plan, with hills or mountains in the middle to divide the layout effectively in two with each side visually isolated from the other.

So the layout design and the appropriate baseboard type for each layout arrangement must be considered together, not in isolation.

One last thought is for N and Z Gauge modellers. The old type of folding card table makes a handy portable solid top layout. A sheet of insulation board can be screwed on top of the original top. However, these little tables are light enough to carry easily, and with the legs folded the layout can be stood against a wall when not in use.

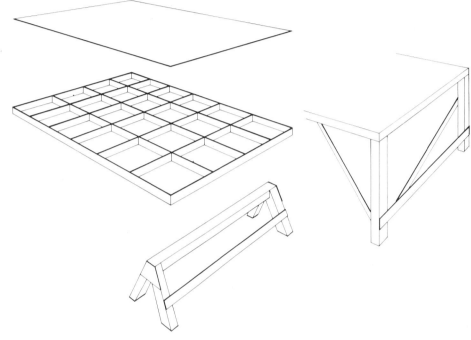

Drawing 5.7: framing for a solid top – 1ft squares for softboard, 2ft squares for chipboard or plywood. Support the board either on legs to the desired height, or on trestles. In the latter case it allows the board to be propped against a wall when not in use

Plywood framing for layouts is a practical alternative to other methods if a power saw is available. The sections can be made to slot together as shown here on the N Gauge Chiltern Green layout of The Model Railway Club

Tracks and track laying

One of the noticeable advances in the model railway hobby in recent years has been the general improvement in the tracks. Train sets and mass market ranges once had sectional clip-together tracks which were 'coarse' in scale, of heavy section and of crude appearance. The alternative, if a modeller wanted track of scale appearance, was to make it from components. Fine realistic results were achieved but it was (and still is) a time-consuming job. All the component parts to make track can still be bought (printed circuit board is popular these days for sleepers), and modellers to the fine P4/S4 standards (and to a certain extent EM) or S Gauge, will still need to make their own track from fine scale components supplied by the specialist firms. There is a certain amount of ready-made EM track to be had, although most EM track will need to be hand-made.

The modern flexible tracks, or the compatible train set tracks, will supply every need and come fully assembled and ready for use. All the major makers produce flexible track in metre or yard lengths, and specialist manufacturers of flexible track include Peco, Atlas, Gem, Rivarossi, Fleisch-

mann, Roco and Hornby. They also all produce sectional track of the 'train set' variety.

While sectional and flexible tracks are available now for all popular scales up to Gauge 1, it is worth looking at some of these gauges in more detail.

OO/HO Track Virtually all ready-made sectional track available for OO/HO Gauge today is compatible make with make, and is to the height known as Code 100 (this is a reference to its depth of rail section: 0·100in – Code 70 is 0·70in and so on). Code 100 track in this scale is actually equivalent to the very heaviest weight of track in real life heavily used main lines. Code 70 or Code 80 tracks are the nearest equivalent to average weight track found in real life. However, Code 100 looks very acceptable and appears much less 'heavy' when it is toned down by weathering. With the exception of wheels to RP25 profile and the old BRSMB 'Scale OO' wheels where the finer flanges are used, Code 100 has to be used with current British and European HO/OO models. Virtually all the makes of sectional track will join up with other makes even if the sleeper spacing

Despite the wide availability of flex-track for the popular gauges, many prefer to lay their own. Here is track construction under way on the O Gauge layout of the Manchester Model Railway Society. On the centre road a train is being used to test accuracy of the finished section, while the adjacent road is still being laid. Note further sections against the wall with sleepers glued in place. All parts (sleepers, rail sections, chairs, or spikes) for track construction are readily available from larger hobby stores

is a little different and the geometry varies. It is difficult to generalise on track and, in any case, it is well illustrated, complete with geometric diagrams, in all the model train catalogues.

However in addition to the individual makers there is in Britain the Peco company whose well-known Streamline range is widely available. This offers flexible track plus a good range of turn-outs to suit virtually all requirements. Peco also make the superior range of sectional track, called Setrack, which is not only sold in the Peco range but also forms the basis for the Mainline and Airfix track systems.

Thus there is no real problem with track other than acquiring what is needed and with careful utilisation even the track which comes in a first train set can be used in all future layouts. Steel, brass and nickel-silver are the various materials from which tracks are made. Steel tends to be used by the mass market manufacturers, but some firms offer steel or nickel-silver, some brass or nickel-silver and some nickel-silver only. Nickel-silver costs a little more than steel, but it is to be commended as the best choice – it has better conductivity, stands up to temperature extremes, and stays cleaner longer. However, any of the materials can be used, and furthermore they can be mixed with each other.

Power connectors are needed to get electricity into the track. Train sets include a terminal rail or a power connector, but if track components are bought separately there is a choice – soldering connections (on a proper permanent layout) or the use of power connectors as before.

All track so far considered is Code 100 with sleepers (cross-ties) which are actually HO size (1:87 scale), even though the track is labelled HO/OO. This will not worry many people as the smaller, closer-spaced sleepers, when used with OO trains, give a somewhat 'finer' look. However, if OO track with sleepers to British (1:76) scale size is required, then the Gem range might appeal. To

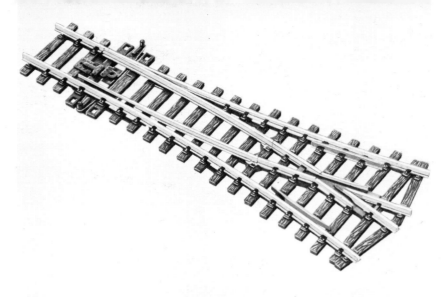

order only, Gem will also supply Code 90 track at no extra cost, giving a finer look.

Another firm worth mentioning is the Japanese maker Shinohara, which offers turn-outs and flex-track in Code 100, and the same range again in Code 70 size for those running American or European trains with RP25 wheels.

Lastly there are some smaller firms, notably Scaleway, which offer flex-track in BRSMB 'fine OO' style with scale bullhead rail. Beyond this is the area of hand-made track.

A recent development is the introduction by Fleischmann of Code 100 sectioned track with realistic plastic ballast built into it.

OO/HO Turn-outs These are considered separately because they could offer more problems than the track itself. All the turn-outs offered in manufacturers' ranges are of the 'dead-frog' type which are the easiest to manage from the point of view of

Peco Y turn-out from the well-known and dependable Streamline range in OO/HO

Uneven track causes stalling. The arrow points to a bad join – a slight dip due to distorted track which causes the wheels to lose contact with the track at this point. If this is not corrected the locomotive is likely to stall every time it reaches this join

Excellent ballasting by the 'bonded ballast' methods on George Reffin's O Gauge garden layout – shown with the track on bare boards in the previous chapter

the electrics. In theory they look after themselves from the control standpoint, and therefore dead frogs are not always the problem they once were.

Another problem is uneven track which can also cause stalling on dead frogs, although this is not so relevant here. Cutting a long story short, the best turn-outs are probably Peco, Setrack or Streamline

(all of which have minimal dead frogs) or Fleischmann. Cases can be put for others, such as Roco, but the Peco and Fleischmann turn-outs seem to give the smoothest ride with the greatest electrical reliability. If they are slightly more expensive than others they are certainly worth it in the long term.

Virtually all turn-outs come as hand-operated

extra wiring is necessary, plus rail breaks to ensure that the track polarity is not reversed and this type of turn-out is really outside the needs of the beginner. Most dead frog turn-outs are selective in that they direct the current along the route selected by the point. This leaves the other route electrically dead, so simplifying wiring or allowing engines to be held 'dead' in sidings. Fleischmann turn-outs can be selective or non-selective for they feature spring clips which can be fitted or removed at will to change the mode. Non-selective turn-outs energise both routes at all times.

Finally, if starting completely from the beginning, with no space problems, there is Conrad HO track, which is made in West Germany. This is a finer scale track (Code 80) already ballasted, but a complete sectional system. However, it has gentle radius curves so needs more space for a given layout than other sectional tracks would take. The ballast and sleepers are arranged so that vehicles with the NEM deep flange will run on the scale section track.

N Gauge Track All the remarks made about OO/HO tracks apply to N Gauge. For a start there are large ranges of flex-track and sectional tracks by Peco, Roco, Minitrix, Shinohara, Arnold and others. The size is Code 80, which is deeper than scale, noticeably so. However there is the Fleischmann Piccolo range as well, and this is very popular not only because of its good electrical reliability but also because it comes ready-ballasted. This looks very realistic and is a great saver from the point of view of time and worry. In general Peco, Fleischmann, Shinohara and Roco turn-outs are the best choice for reliability in this crucial area.

A recent development is the introduction of Code 50 N Gauge track by Peco and this gives a much finer and better look than the old 'heavy' Code 80 rail.

O Gauge Track Several firms offer sectional O track which is similar in style to OO/HO track except for its size, mostly Code 124. In addition Peco offer flex-track and turn-outs in their Streamline series, and many others produce trade components and turn-out kits for both 'fine' and 'coarse' scale track standards. Making track by hand in this scale is rather easier than in smaller scales, simply because the parts are bigger and easier to handle. Therefore it is probably true to say that more Gauge O workers make their own track than those working in smaller scales.

Gauge 1 Track Märklin offer excellent flat-bottom track of German style in sectional form and made of stainless steel so that it can also be used outdoors. Tenmille and Peco make flex-track, again in similar style to the smaller scales. As with O Gauge, modellers will be dependent on specialist stockists or the larger hobby shops for supplies.

Z Gauge Märklin produce a full range of sectional track while Peco produce Streamline flex-track and turn-outs, all of which matches the Märklin track.

TT Gauge Track in sectional form is made by

items. Various mechanical levers and frames for remote operation can be bought or turn-outs can be motorised for electrical remote operation.

Peco Streamline also offer 'live-frog' turn-outs, as do Gem. These have electrical conductivity right through the point, so the stalling problem due to loss of power on the pick-up is avoided. However,

Mark out the track position very carefully before it is removed for ballasting. Note that sectional and flexible tracks fit happily together, as can be seen here where Fleischmann sectional pieces are being used with Peco Streamline turn-outs and flex-track

Berliner-Bahn of East Germany. Bemo of West Germany make 12mm gauge track for HOm narrow gauge but it is also suitable for TT, while Gem in Great Britain make flex-track.

Narrow Gauges For all the narrow gauge scales it is possible to use the appropriate track originally intended for standard gauge models. Thus 16·5mm OO/HO track can be used for On16·5, and N Gauge track for HOe or OO9. Gauge O track can be used for SM32 and so on. The sleepers (cross-ties) are too close together when used like this, for the scale of standard gauge track is, of course, different to the narrow gauge scale. The ruse used to overcome this problem is to add plenty of ballast to conceal the under-scale sleepers as much as possible so that the close spacing is not too apparent.

However, specialist track makers Peco produce narrow gauge track which has correct scale sleepers for OO9/HOe, On16 and SM32. This is sold under the name 'Crazy Track' reflecting the rather rough ragged look of typical narrow gauge sleepers. Bemo also produce HOe and HOm track with correctly

scaled sleepers while Shinohara and others produce a range of track to 10·5mm gauge for American narrow gauge, HOn 3.

Home-built Track Building and laying track is quite straightforward and firms like Peco, Bonds, Studiolith, and others make all the necessary components, gauges, and tools for those who wish to lay track to suit a particular location, and, for example, sweeping transitional curves can be built to follow exactly individual requirements. In P4/S4, the fine scale equivalent of OO, or OOO, the fine scale equivalent of N, there is no option but to make the track. However, Studiolith, who produce P4 track, can supply everything needed, including templates and jigs. In the case of EM there is some flex-track available from the firm of Scaleway, and some firms offer assembled turn-outs. Ratio make sleeper bases in plastic for EM and this is useful, for the EM rail section slides into the sleepers to make easily assembled track.

Today the mass of modellers working in the popular scales use flex-track or even sectional track, or a combination of the two for they are compatible with each other in OO/HO, N, and Z Gauges.

Working Out the Track Plan Once the baseboard is complete a start can be made in putting the track down. This is another one of those times when it is all too easy to rush too quickly ahead, obtain the track, and put it on the board without a second thought, until trains are run and then some of the sidings and other arrangements prove to be impracticable.

Experience can prove the fact that a plan already published does not necessarily mean that it can be made to fit the same area exactly. Sometimes published plans are slightly theoretical in that the designer has no particular make of turn-out in mind. As turn-out lengths can vary from make to make, what may appear in print as a good place for a siding if one radius of track is used may turn out to be physically impossible using another make of turn-out. One way to ensure that everything fits the baseboard before buying turn-outs and track is to use either the templates made by the various major track manufacturers or stencils which some of the other manufacturers also supply.

In the case of Peco, OO/HO Gauge, O Gauge and N Gauge turn-outs, templates are available to match each type produced. The Hornby range of templates are similar and other makes are available on which the templates are simply drawn out full-size on paper. These printed templates can simply be cut out and it can then be seen how turn-outs will fit any given track plan without the expense of buying the turn-out first. For example, from just one or two templates it may be possible to work out the number of left-hand and right-hand turn-outs, and which radii are required, so that a 'shopping list' for all the major track components required for a layout can be prepared.

The cut out templates can be pinned straight onto a baseboard surface, although if changes are to be made this could be confusing, so another approach is to pin ordinary shelf lining paper over the baseboard surface, then pin or tape (with masking tape) the turn-out or templates to the lining paper and draw round them. A section of flexible track can be used as a template to mark out the sections of railway between the various turn-outs. The end result, in effect, is a full-size drawn-out plan of the layout, and it then becomes an easy matter then to obtain the exact amount of track required.

Full-sized templates also mean that such matters as siding lengths and loop line capacities can be tested without laying any track at all. The full-sized templates give a very accurate picture of finished appearance – rolling stock can be placed on a marked out siding to test the capacity. All too often modellers produce layouts with sidings which are hardly worthwhile because they turn out to have a capacity for only one or two vehicles, which tends to look unrealistic. Another important advantage of full-sized templates is that clearances for platform edges and sidings and '6ft ways' can also be checked to ensure that locomotives or coaches will not obstruct buildings placed near the track or side swipe each other as they pass.

Just as it is important to have firm level strong baseboards which will not buckle or cause other troubles so it is equally vital that track is laid with extreme care. Badly laid track will, of course, cause derailments. The key to a layout which works efficiently and well is perfect track laying on a good strong baseboard. Track laying seems easy enough if one starts with the components of a train set, or the sectional track that comes with such sets and is available separately: simply clip the track together, lay it on the board, pin it down and run the trains. However, this has an immediate visual failing in that it has no ballast which is the normal feature of all real trackage. Similarly, while the track is clipped together and comes in sectional form there are usually no problems with the electrics or the actual running of the rolling stock on the rails. However, even with sectional track there will be problems unless it is laid extremely carefully. For example it is all too easy to slide two track sections together and miss the adjacent web of one side of the track. This means that the track lies on top of the connector on one side. From a normal viewing position all may look well but as soon as a train runs along it it meets a slight step in the rail join and may well be derailed. The fact that the rail connectors are not completely joined up may also mean that there is a break in the circuit and the train will not run at all. A first golden rule, therefore, is to ensure that all connections between adjacent sections of track are firmly and carefully made. If a rail connector is bent or buckled it is far better to discard it and fit another since rail connectors are not expensive yet they are one of the keys to good electrical conductivity.

It is surprisingly easy to visually misjudge a rail connection and there have been several occasions where time has been spent pinning down track to a baseboard only for the modeller to find that one of the connections is badly made. As often as not this can only be corrected by lifting all or most of the track again. Allied to the care in ensuring that the track connectors are properly fitted is the need to ensure that adjacent track sections are butted properly in line with each other. It is also extremely easy to put slight pressure on a track section to make it join at one end and in doing so cause it to be pulled away slightly from the next section of track so that there is no longer a smooth transition between the joins at that end of the track. This may, in fact, be an almost imperceptible distortion but it could cause trains to jerk or jump as they cross the gap.

Therefore when making any connection between two adjacent sections of track a second golden rule is to ensure that the line of the connection is perfectly done with no distortion or bend at the rail joint. This is a deceptive matter, for looking down on the track it may appear to be perfectly lined up. The real test is to look along the track at eye level, when any kinks caused by bad joins will be immediately apparent.

These days most sectional tracks match in basic geometry so that the makes can be mixed to some extent if desired. The same applies to sectional track sold on the American and European markets although the geometries are not necessarily the same. Most of the track which comes in train sets is made of steel but some manufacturers produce sectional track in brass. Other leading manufacturers produce their sectional track in nickel silver. It is worth pointing out, however, that steel, nickel silver, and even brass tracks can be mixed together quite happily so long as they are all kept clean, although it is best to keep to one material.

Sectional track has limitations and one of these is that the curves are all to relatively sharp radius. Usually there are at least two radii to every sectional track system to enable double track curves to be laid. For OO/HO the curve is relatively sharp and could be between 13 and 18in (330 and 457mm) radius, depending on the make. This sharp radius of curvature is advantageous for putting a layout into a small area but such curves are far sharper than the prototype, except perhaps for full-size tramway and dockyard lines. Therefore for a bigger layout where more realistic sweeping curves are required the enthusiast prefers to use flexible trackage systems of which Peco Streamline, Atlas Customline, or Shinohara are probably the best known. In all cases except the very small Z Gauge, flexible track itself is sold in yards or metre lengths. Most of the other major manufacturers of sectional track also produce flexible track sections of similar type and in some cases they also produce larger radius turn-outs.

Using flexible track of the Streamline type and associated turn-outs, means that a layout is no longer limited to the very formal geometry of sectional track and can therefore look much more realistic than the type of layout which uses train set track. Whether train set type sectional track or flexible track is used the recommended procedures for track laying are exactly the same. It is quite possible to mix sectional track components with flexible track and indeed for very sharp curves, it is probably easier to use sectional track than to put a severe curve into flexible track. Similarly turn-outs such as those from the Setrack range can be used with ordinary Streamline flexible track.

Obviously the mix of track will really depend on

the layout plan. On a large layout or a wall hugger layout where gentle radius curves are feasible then it is probably best to go for flexible track throughout. Essentially the larger the radius of the curve the more realistic a layout will look and the better the stock will run – long coaches on sharp radius curves look extremely ugly and unrealistic, due to the overhang and the displacement of the bogies, trucks and couplers.

Ballasting It has already been remarked that for realism the track should be ballasted. There are several ways of ballasting track and the most readily available is foam ballast inlay. This is made by Peco to fit the Streamline range of track but can also be used with other tracks which have the same sleeper spacing, while Hornby make foam inlay and so do a few other firms, certainly in the popular scales. There is even a foam ballast inlay for Gauge 1 to fit Märklin track. All these inlays are moulded in browns or greys to resemble ballast colour.

Laying track with foam ballast inlay is quite simple so long as care is taken. Start with the most complex point work on the layout, which is often around a main station, and simply join as many basic sections together as possible. For example, facing turn-outs which form a cross-over can simply be put together with rail joiners. Using sectional track everything will go together quite quickly, although it may be necessary to play around with a few short straights or curves in order to get a chosen track formation together without straining the pieces or leaving gaps or ugly kinks in the layout. With flexible tracks one literally just curves them gently in the fingers and measures off the distance for each section. As it is curved the inner rail naturally starts to protrude, then with a fine razor-saw the excess lengths can simply be trimmed to fit. Should there be any roughness use a small file to clean up

the burrs. Add the rail joiners and the job is done. Keep looking along the track at rail level to ensure that there are no kinks in the connections. The whole lot fits quite snugly into the foam ballast inlay, which is naturally trimmed to match the track. Where there are long lengths of track without turn-outs the track can simply be put into the foam inlay and the whole lot flexed together. Before dropping the track into place brush white PVA glue along the entire length under the sleepers to hold track and ballast together.

When laying track in position, occasional rail pins can be put through the appropriate sleepers (they will push easily into the softboard base). If the glueing is done carefully, however, few pins will be needed and they should not be pushed hard home. Naturally a power unit, locomotive and some stock should be available so that the circuit clearances at sidings, run-around loops and crossings can be checked. If double track is laid, the longest vehicles should be tried on the two tracks to ensure there is no 'side-swiping'. Keep trying the circuit by running trains over every join, turn-out and siding, to locate faults as work proceeds. If a loco stalls on turn-outs it *could* be the fault of the loco, but quite often it is due to a slight twist in the rail or a badly fitting frog which causes a wheel to lift very slightly from the track and so lose power. Judicious use of track pins will often flatten out a slightly warped turn-out. If a turn-out seems suspect try finger pressure on the sleeper ends one side or other. If this restores the power, put in a pin or two on that side.

The other important point to mention is weathering. On real track the rail, and very often the sleepers too, take on a brownish colour – a mix of rust and dirt. Only the rail surface is worn and bright. To get this effect in miniature the track must be painted with 'rail colour', readily available in most paint ranges. Dark earth is an alternative shade

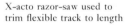

X-acto razor-saw used to trim flexible track to length

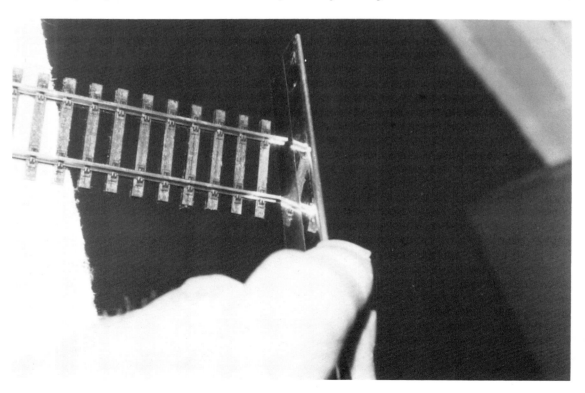

to use. When using foam ballast inlay the easiest procedure is to paint all the track after it is cut to length but before it is finally glued into the inlay and positioned. It is easy enough, although a little time consuming, to paint all the track carefully (*repeat* carefully) so that no paint is allowed to run inside fishplates, electrical terminals or the adjoining faces of moving stock rails in turn-outs.

Paint is a great insulator and if it gets anywhere where current runs electrical problems could result. The top surfaces of the rails should be wiped clean as work proceeds, and when all work is complete a track cleaner block (sold by most model shops) will restore the bright surface. If paint runs inadvertently inside any rail connector remove it, clean the rail end, and put on a new connector. Before finally fixing down the track test it all over once again with locomotives and stock.

This may sound tedious and pedantic, but careful work and constant checking throughout the track-laying process will pay handsome dividends later on.

Painting the track can take several evenings depending on layout size. It takes at least an evening's work on even the smallest layout. It can be frustrating to find later that there are bright bits of unpainted metal, so be prepared to have a few extra sessions touching in gaps later on. Some modellers overcome these problems by not weathering the track at all, leaving it bright and shiny, although

shiny tracks do not look at all realistic, for even freshly laid tracks in real life are rusty due to outside storage.

Foam ballast inlay offers a good and well-cushioned ride for trains, but it does look exceptionally clean and uniform, which is fine for well maintained main lines but does not satisfy all modellers. In addition, when foam ballast inlay is used on portable layouts – which might spend much time propped against walls – experience has shown a tendency for the track to part company from the ballast, however well it seems to be glued and pinned.

So what are the alternatives? The method preferred and much used by the author is 'clean' and kind to the electrics which is the all-important consideration. This is a system sold by the German firm of Arnold for N Gauge and Noch for Z Gauge but readily adaptable to TT and OO/HO Gauges. It uses PVC tape attached sticky side up under the sleepers, then sprinkled with cork ballast which adheres to the sticky surface of the tape. The Arnold ballast is particularly realistic and correctly coloured, but any fine cork ballast can be used, including the natural colour variety, sold cheaply in model shops. In this case paint the track *and* the ballast together after all track laying is complete. If using Arnold or any other pre-coloured ballast paint the track before laying as for the foam inlay method.

Painting track while in position prior to ballasting by the PVC strip method. Also shown here is a Fleischmann power connector which is efficient and inconspicuous in use

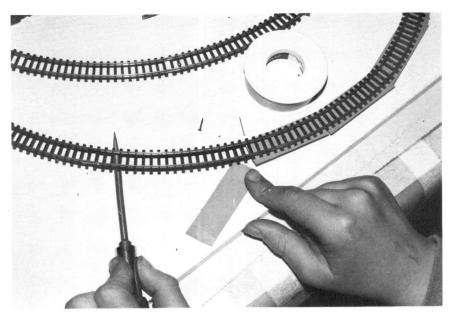

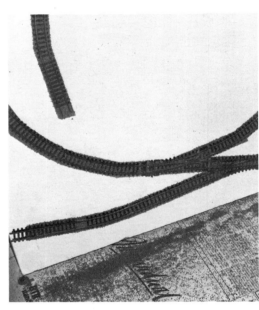

This sequence of pictures shows the stages of ballasting track using PVC tape and cork ballast. Lengths of tape are placed under the track, the ballast is tamped down on the sticky tape with fingers and a stiff brush, the loose ballast is tipped off on to newspaper (for re-use later) and the job is done. This is N Gauge but the same procedure is followed for Z, TT, or OO/HO

Although Arnold and Noch produce complete ballasting kits, grey or brown PVC tape can be purchased separately for use with other makes of ballast (the 38mm wide roll is required for OO/HO tracks). With this method of ballasting the track is pinned firmly to the baseboard so that it will not spring away – ideal for a fold-away or portable layout which stands on its side. If the track is to stand on shouldered ballast, as on a main line, cut strips of $\frac{1}{16}$ in or $\frac{1}{8}$ in (1·6mm or 3mm) balsa to the required width for the track gauge, bevel the edges, and sandwich the balsa strips between the baseboard and the PVC tape when pinning down. Because the tape may curl up over the bevel, however, run some PVA glue along the bevel and glue the edges of the tape down. Alternatively pin the edges of the tape to the bevel, using ordinary track pins. For double track and so forth just keep adding extra widths of PVC tape. Leave a strip clear of tape under all tie-bars of turn-outs. The advantage of this method is that it does not involve glue or hard ballast chips and because it is only pinned down it is very easy to lift

track for later alterations or maintenance without damage. Just rip the tape from under the sleepers.

Next comes a variation of this idea, a self-adhesive PVC strip which is sold in rolls. Various makes are available, one being Stick-a-Track. The strip is about $\frac{1}{8}$in thick. Some makes are adhesive on both sides, others on top only. The strip is cut to appropriate lengths and the track is stuck on top of it, and curved as required. After lightly pinning in position loose ballast chippings are sprinkled over the strip and worked in, adhering to the sticky surface to give a shouldered ballast effect. The strip is cut up to form the appropriate shapes for turn-outs and cross-overs. Again this is a 'clean' system which does not affect the electrics, but it is more 'permanent' than the PVC tape system. In theory it is removable and re-usable, although in practice it holds the track quite tightly and the track can possibly be damaged or twisted if it is lifted again after laying. For weathering it can be painted before laying, or track and ballast can be painted together after laying is complete.

A recent development has been Styroplast ballast strip, made in West Germany. This consists of an expanded polystyrene foam strip moulded to hold the sleepers. A covering of realistic ballast is provided, together with optional shouldered edges which can be removed as desired. The ballast strip curves to accommodate flex-track and is available to suit the leading makes. Separate moulded ballast bases are produced to suit turn-outs. Overall this is a realistic and clean system – track needs pre-painting if weathered – although it costs a little more than other systems.

All these systems are 'artificial' in that they depend on some sort of plastic base. A very realistic solution to the ballasting system is called 'bonded ballasting'. Here the cork or granite ballast chippings are tipped over the track and a brush is used to sweep the ballast into shape around the sleepers. At this stage all the ballast is loose – just like the real thing. Next a dropper or spray is used to squirt a wetting agent (water with a drop of liquid detergent) over the ballast. While this is still wet a dropper is used to spread either matt medium acrylic varnish (sold in art shops) or diluted PVA glue all over the ballast. This runs through the ballast and sets, holding all the ballast in place with no visible adhesive due to its transparent nature. The system is simple but a major caution must be stressed – turn-outs should be treated with the greatest care, for using

Above: on the layout of Sid Stubbs of Manchester the hand-laid track is on a cork sheet ballast base over which coarse sand is glued to give a realistic effect of well compressed ballast. Note that the track is fully weathered

Styroplast ballast inlay is an alternative to foam ballast inlay

this system it is only too easy to gum them solid, completely defeating all track-laying efforts! It is suggested that the areas around the moving parts of turn-outs should be left bare of ballast. When all the bonding is complete go back to the turn-outs and carefully glue ballast into the gaps so that there is no chance of the moving parts being obstructed.

There are other ways of ballasting, covered in books and magazines. The old traditional method was to smear glue along the track bed area, lay the track on it, and drop ballast over the track while the glue is still wet. The whole lot sets solid and permanent, which is fine but it means the track cannot be lifted and used again if the layout is altered later. Also there is the same risk of gumming up the moving parts of turn-outs. Therefore this system has little to commend it when 'cleaner' methods are available.

It should be mentioned that with Conrad or Fleischmann track in OO/HO or Fleischmann track in N Gauge, all the ballasting is done as part of the track, so the methods of depicting ballast described above can be ignored.

Turn-out Operation Turn-out control will vary with requirements. In their simplest form (in miniature and in real life) turn-outs are hand thrown from a lever alongside the moving stock rails. Most model turn-outs have a tag which can be switched with the finger to change direction of the rails, while a spring holds the stock rails in place. On a simple layout depicting a branch line there may be nothing more than hand-thrown turn-outs.

To improve on the hand switch which operates the tie-bar of the turn-out, it is possible to instal a miniature point lever alongside the turn-out, as in full-size practice. Various styles are available and they are used with a short 20 or 22 gauge wire joining the lever to the tie-bar of the turn-out (not all makes of turn-out have provision for fitting a wire however). There is usually an omega loop in the wire to give the required degree of 'spring', and ready-made omega wires are available from suppliers such as Gem. It is necessary to adjust the throw of the lever by centring the lever vertically while the point blades are in the midway position, after which the lever unit is pinned in place.

The next refinement is the 'wire in tube' system of remote control. Here a moving piano wire inside a tube is used to give movement to the blades. The tube is carried to the baseboard edge and attached to a lever frame. The tubing can be curved to change direction, turning down to about 2in (51mm) radius to do so. Firms like Gem and W & T produce this 'wire in tube' material. It is possible to lead wires from several turn-outs, say in a station area, to one position on the baseboard where they can be linked to a bank of lever frames as in a real mechanical signal box. Indeed, it is a favourite ploy to hide the lever frame inside a model signal box from which the back is removed to give access to operate the lever. Where a signal box is not available, lever frames can be hidden inside or behind other suitable lineside buildings.

Electrical control of turn-outs is even more popular, and on a large layout it is the most convenient method to use. Makers like Roco, Hornby,

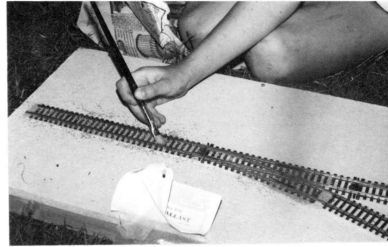

Märklin, Fleischmann and others produce quite slender point motors which clip on the sides of their regular manual turn-outs to convert them to remote control, while other firms make turn-outs in electrical control form as an alternative to manual turn-outs. All these point motors are mounted above the baseboard adjacent to the turn-out. After installation, they can be covered in ballast (but take care with the glue) to look like a ballast heap alongside the track, or flock powder can be used to make the motor look like a grassy bank. All makers give a good instruction sheet showing how their particular point motors are installed.

For 'invisible' point motors one must turn to specialist firms which produce efficient little moving solenoid motors which fit under the baseboard immediately below the turn-out they control. A vertical lever pulls the tie-bar back and forth as the current slaps the solenoids back and forth to switch the turn-outs. Here we see the need for thorough pre-planning, for if these motors are to be used under the baseboard a slot needs to be cut under each turn-out with a keyhole saw, and clearly this must be done after positioning but before finally ballasting the track. These point motors can be installed on the surface adjacent to the turn-out, but then they will have to be disguised under lineside huts as they are very obtrusive.

All these turn-out motors work from the ac current output which is provided for accessory operation

Ballasting track with Tracklay (and similar systems). The trackbed roll is stuck under the track, crushed granite ballast is distributed by brush or fingers, the next section is pinned in place as work proceeds, the shoulders (edges) of the ballast are glued separately with loose ballast, and the completed work is ready for weathering with paint brush or sprayed paint, wiping off the running surfaces before the paint dries

Realistic ballasting on Vic Hart's 1:32 scale narrow gauge layout using the basic method of sprinkling granulated cork or crushed granite ballast over glue as the track is laid

on all but the cheapest power units; 16–20 volts ac, with an output of 2–3 amps is best, and 3 amps should ensure positive action of the solenoid. If a power unit lacks this output then a separate ac transformer can be used instead. Great care is needed when installing these point motors as wires and switches are called for. Check the motor for free movement before it is fitted and oil it if necessary to ensure that the solenoids switch right across, far enough to actually switch the turn-out. The throw is minimal with point blades but it is important that everything works efficiently – for example that the points actually switch fully, and that the switch movement is done with sufficient force to maintain electrical integrity through the point. Therefore, the motor must be lined up correctly with no binding on the operating arms.

Lastly, another matter of pre-planning: ensure that where insulated rail joiners are required (for

example to isolate an engine shed road) they are fitted first as it is difficult to change after all ballasting is finished!

Crossing Baseboard Joints If the advice given in the previous chapter is followed with a large baseboard in a number of sections, to facilitate either portability or later changes, a problem arises when the tracks cross the join in adjacent baseboard sections. There are a number of ways to deal with this. For a start, if a layout is of a permanent nature, bolted together in sections but not likely to be moved, the track can be taken right across the join without any sort of break. This is convenient electrically, but one has to remember to saw through the track at the join with a razor-saw should the baseboards ever be dismantled. This may cause inconvenience when the layout is re-erected, but can be minimised if one follows the rest of the recognised rules for crossing baseboard joins.

Essentially these are measures to be taken if a layout has any sort of portability or transportability. First need is a gap in the rails at the baseboard join, so it is essential to keep the track formation as simple as possible here – avoid having turn-outs, crossings, or buffers at joins. Keep to straight or only gently curved track, crossing the join. Leave it unballasted immediately each side of the join. Each side of the join put in a brass round-headed screw so that the head touches the underneath of each rail. In other words four screws, two each side of the join. Solder the rail to the screws, then saw a gap in the rails in line with the baseboard join. Electrical continuity can be assured by soldering a wire to each screw under the board and using a plug and socket to join them up – or even twisting the bare ends together. An alternative to screws is a brass strip soldered under each rail end and bent over the edge of each baseboard section. The springiness of the brass strips will cause them to touch when the sections are bolted together. Simplest of all, arrange the track so that a short sectional straight or curve crosses the gap, and do not pin this to the board or the ballast. Put the rail joiners on this short track section. When the two boards are bolted together, drop the track

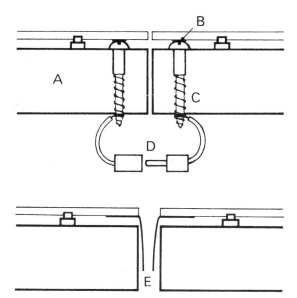

Drawing 6.1: two alternative methods, using round-headed screws or brass strips, to ensure electrical continuity across baseboard joins.
(A) Baseboard; (B) Solder; (C) Screw; (D) Plug and socket; (E) Brass strips soldered under rail, touch when baseboard sections meet

section into place and use a small screwdriver to slide the rail joiners along to join up with the adjacent track each side of the gap. The only requirement here is careful measurement to get the correct spacing for the track section.

The simplest method of carrying track across a baseboard join is to use a separate half-section of sectional track, sliding the joiners into place with the tip of a screwdriver. Careful measurement is needed to get the distance accurate between the ends of the pinned down track on the two boards. Note the loose sleeper which is slid into place in the gap

Basic wiring and control

The model railway hobby can be as complex or as simple as one cares to make it, a fact stressed several times already in this book. When it comes to the matter of electrics and control systems some would-be modellers take fright and perhaps do not try even to make a layout, but keep their trains as shelf display items. It seems to them that anything involving electrical wiring *must* be complicated.

Certainly some of the grander layouts seen at exhibitions or described in magazines look complicated behind the control panel, and somebody with no electrical training might doubt his ability in this department. But even a complete novice need have no fears about getting the trains running, for a layout can be tailored to match electrical knowledge, just as it can be tailored to space or money, or a favourite scale. For those who want to go deeply into the subject complete books are available; here we will keep everything quite simple, covering just what is needed to know to get a layout started.

First to elementary principles. The bulk of today's miniature railway systems are electrically operated, although there is a little live steam in Gauge O, Gauge 1, and even occasionally in OO, while some clockwork (spring drive) may also be encountered. With few exceptions, electric model trains use a 12 volt dc (direct current) system, with the two running rails acting as the current carriers. Power comes from the domestic supply and passes through the power/control unit to reduce it from domestic voltage to the safe 12 volt dc. Most train sets these days come with a power unit (and wiring instructions), while there are some excellent power units available from specialist makers. Although some power units are more sophisticated than others they all do the same basic job. Cheaper train sets come with battery controllers which work off 12 volt dc dry cells. The degree of speed control with these is generally not so good, although a battery controller allows model trains to be run even when there is no mains electricity supply.

DC Power Units The modern power unit contains a rectifier to change the mains alternating current (ac) to direct current (dc) – in countries where this is necessary – and a transformer to reduce the mains voltage to 12 volts. There is a speed and direction control, which is based on a variable resistance in the most common power units. This system of speed control has some inherent limitations, notably in the uneven performance of the locomotive, which requires careful adjustment of the speed control knob on gradients and in a tendency for the motor to race away at starts. A slightly more

Most manufacturers now offer control panel sections which can be made to depict a modeller's own layout. This is the Lima version with electric pencil probe which activates the circuit

Opposite: a more elaborate control panel used on the Gladstone Yard hump shunting layout of Manchester MRS. All turnout switches and isolating switches are in the necessary positions on the track diagram

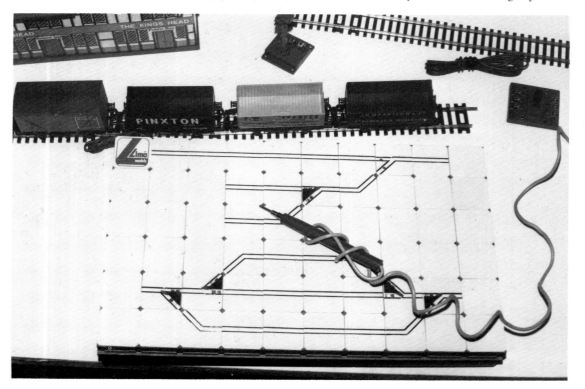

sophisticated type of power unit helps overcome such problems with what is called 'half wave rectification' and variable resistance (high and low). Half wave gives only half the wave cycle so that at starting only intermittent pulses of power are fed to the motor giving slower, smoother turn-over. Most of the power units made by the big model train firms

are of the basic type (without half wave) while specialist control unit makers offer the slightly superior units with half wave.

More recently transistorised power units have been developed, giving a constant output and using

modern electronic techniques to simulate braking, inertia (simulated momentum), and auto-power regulation, which adapts the controller to the differing characteristics of different makes of motor. Braking effects and acceleration typical of the type

of loco being controlled can be simulated with these power units.

Despite these options, however, most of the quite simple units supplied with train sets will still give good service, at least for early efforts. If starting off by buying components rather than a train set, then the well-proven H & M Clipper would be a good choice.

Connecting Up Whichever power unit is used, there are basically just two wires from the output terminals taking the power to the track. Some makes of track actually have terminal rails – lengths of track with clips or screw terminals to which the wire leads from the power unit are attached. More commonly today separate clip-on connectors are sold which enable the leads to be taken to any convenient part of the track, and are also much less conspicuous. These leads can be soldered to the outside webs of the rails. This is the method used on exhibition layouts and more advanced layouts, and is also advocated in books and magazines. Lack of soldering experience need not be a worry. With a basic train set oval the wire leads will just run straight from the power unit to the track. With even the simplest layout, however, most modellers will want to conceal those ugly wires from view and this is done by drilling a small hole (or holes) through the baseboard adjacent to the power feed position and tacking or clipping the wires neatly under the baseboard and leading them back to the control position at the edge of the board, wherever that happens to be.

So long as a layout is a single track oval or a single track end-to-end that is all one needs to do. Very simply, with the 12 volt dc system the locomotive picks up power from one rail through its wheels on one side, this drives the motor, and the power is returned through the other rail. Sometimes the tender wheels also pick up, and sometimes the bogies do as well – it depends on the design. The wheels are insulated from each other, of course, to prevent short circuiting.

The question of power and control is a key one, for poor electrics cause most frustration when it comes to building and operating a layout, and more people give up because of this than for any other single reason. Nothing is more annoying than a good-looking locomotive that falters for no apparent reason or fails to run through a turn-out without stalling.

Such problems can be overcome, with a good locomotive for a start, choosing from magazine reports, trial runs in shops, or commendation from friends. Certain makes have good reputations built up over many years, among them Arnold, Roco, Liliput, Fleischmann, Minitrix and Athearn, while the most recent Hornby and British Lima locomotives are good in this respect also. The next step is to ensure everything is kept clean. Running models on track set up temporarily on a carpet or table cloth does them no good – fluff gets into the mechanism and gears. Clean all mechanisms, pick-ups, wheels and brushes from time to time and follow the loco maker's oiling instructions. Locomotives should not be taken apart, however, unless absolutely necessary (to replace brushes for example) and there are modern cleaners today such as Peco Electroclean, which are simply squirted into the mechanism from underneath and work wonders. Personal observation suggests that locos with rubber traction tyres give more trouble than those without, although this has to be something of a generalisation. Locos without traction tyres, and with as many pick-up wheels as possible, should give minimal trouble. Personal experience, again, leads to the conclusion that Athearn, Roco, Liliput and Fleischmann locomotives give performances superior to most others in

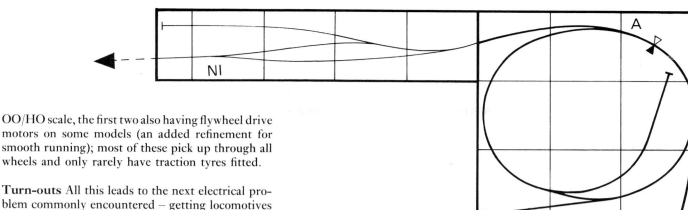

OO/HO scale, the first two also having flywheel drive motors on some models (an added refinement for smooth running); most of these pick up through all wheels and only rarely have traction tyres fitted.

Turn-outs All this leads to the next electrical problem commonly encountered – getting locomotives through turn-outs. The turn-outs sold with virtually all sectional trackage systems plus the original Peco Streamline, Atlas and Shinohara turn-outs are of the 'dead frog' variety. The frog is the actual point where the second routes of the turn-out diverges from the original direction. If the rails are live throughout it can be seen that the right-hand rail of the second route would touch the left-hand rail of the original route and as the left-hand rail is of opposite polarity to the right-hand rail a short circuit would result. By making the frog segment in plastic (ie, electrically 'dead') this shorting is prevented. Wires carried under the plastic 'dead frog' ensure continuity of the current on both routes as necessary. A loco passing over the dead frog may stall if it has insufficient electrical pick-ups (these are, of course, ineffective as they pass over the dead frog). A loco with insufficient pick-ups may be carried over the frog by its own momentum if moving fast and then pick up again, but the same loco crawling slowly over the frog may stall. The answer, naturally, is to select locos with plenty of pick-ups, which most recent models have, so that some pick-up wheels are always on live track. Obviously the smaller the dead frog the less the risk of stalling, which makes Peco turn-outs better than most, with Fleischmann and Roco also good in this respect.

The other matter to watch for is a perfectly flat turn-out. Inspect all dead frogs very carefully. Sometimes they stand slightly proud of the rail, or slightly below, forming an almost imperceptible 'step' which causes the loco to lurch, perhaps lifting wheels from the track – again a stalled locomotive is the result.

Finally, test each turn-out for electrical integrity. The moving point blades should snap firmly against the rails and contact springs. Sometimes there is very slight warping in the turn-out which affects the contact surface and the turn-out appears dead. This can be checked by putting light finger pressure on each side of the turn-out in turn, when a stalled loco may start moving again. Pins into the sleepers on the affected side very often cure this particular problem, but if all else fails replace the turn-out.

Keep it Simple Returning now to wiring the layout, anyone who wants to go no further than plugging in two wires can progress happily in the hobby without ever doing more than that, provided a layout is not very big and not too complicated. It is particularly true if a layout is based on an oval of

track with just a few sidings and single line throughout. The secret really lies in the dead frog turn-outs. For these come in two styles – selective or non-selective (or isolating or non-isolating). With isolating turn-outs current only passes in the direction the points are set. Thus a siding or loop is isolated if the turn-outs are set down the main road. Hence a loco can be held in the siding or loop while another loco runs elsewhere on the layout, so there is a degree of sectionalisation with no other effort than ensuring that the turn-outs are all in first class working order.

With the non-isolating turn-out, power is carried along both routes at all times no matter which direction is set. Thus judicious use of isolating and non-isolating turn-outs will even by-pass the need for extra power feeds even in 'kick-back' sidings which appear to be facing in the opposite direction to the power feed.

On the layout shown in drawing 7.1, small and compact as OO/HO goes – even so it runs up to 10ft (3m) in two directions – the trains will run with only the one power feed marked. All the turn-outs in the drawing are marked NI if they are non-isolating. It can be seen that those in loops and 'kick-back' sidings furthest from the power feed are all non-isolating and a loco will shunt back into the sidings even when the turn-outs appear to be set against the direction of current.

Of course there are limitations to such simplicity, the major one being that only one loco can actually be moving at one time. But for a branch line or short line, or light railway, this is no hardship. Other locos not in use are parked in isolated sidings and only one engine is brought out at a time. This should not be dismissed as over-simple, for although such a layout is technically limited, this ultra-simple wiring is no hardship at all on a small, semi-portable branch layout which fits in a bedroom or small apartment.

Naturally even a layout as small as the Willow Valley (illustrated) can be sectionalised in a more sophisticated way, complete with more than one power feed and with sectional sidings. Drawing 7.2 shows the idea. All the wiring for the rail breaks and the power feeds is taken back to a control panel and a possible position for this is shown.

Almost any very small layout, 6ft × 4ft (1·80m × 1·20m) or smaller (in OO/HO) can be wired in this very simple way so long as the track plan is simple

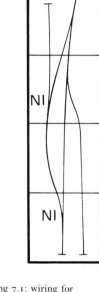

Drawing 7.1: wiring for Willow Valley layout (1). (A) Power feed; (NI) Non-isolating turn-out

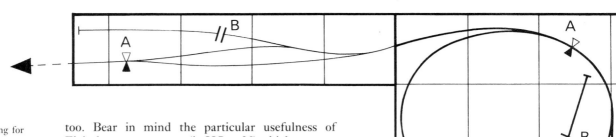

Drawing 7.2: wiring for
Willow Valley layout (2).
(A) Power feed; (B) Isolating
gap (rail break) with switch;
(C) Control panel

too. Bear in mind the particular usefulness of Fleischmann turn-outs (in HO or N) which come as non-isolating turn-outs with small clips which carry the current to do this. Remove these clips and the turn-out is instantly converted to an isolating version. These clips can be used with other makes of isolating turn-out to convert them to the non-isolating variety.

The golden rule for dead frog turn-outs is always feed the power to the toe of the point. This applies to any number of turn-outs so long as they all face away from the power feed. But a kick-back siding in drawing 7.3 needs a second power feed if isolated turn-outs are used at a cross-over so that a loco can run into the kick-back siding once the cross-over turn-outs are set for the main line, thus isolating the siding. But note that if non-isolating turn-outs are used the kick-back siding can be operated with no extra power feed so long as there is no train running elsewhere on the layout at the time.

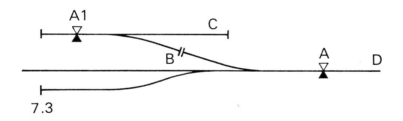

7.3

Key to Drawings 7.3 – 7.8:
(A) Power feed; (A1) Second
power feed; (B) Isolating
gap (rail break) with switch;
(C) Kick-back siding;
(D) Mainline; (E) On/off
switch; (F) Dead section
when switched off;
(G) Power unit; (G1) Power
unit 2; (H) Common return;
(J) Double-pole double-
throw switch.
Lower part of drawing 7.5
shows cross over with live
frog

Live Frog Turn-outs To overcome the stalling problems (or risk of these), 'live frog' turn-outs were introduced (called Electrofrog by Peco, who also call their dead frog turn-outs Insulfrog). Peco, Shinohara and Gem all offer these, as do more specialist makers like Scaleway, while all the finer scale turn-outs of the home-made variety, such as those for P4/S4 or EM are of this type. Because there is metal right through the frog (hence 'live frog') the current is not interrupted in the running rails and risks of stalling are eliminated. But because all the live rails are in contact, depending on how the point is switched, there will be conflicting polarity in the running rails, leading to short circuits if measures are not taken to stop it. Drawing 7.4 shows why.

To overcome this problem it is necessary to put insulated gaps in the rails, and all feeds must be to the toe of the frog. Drawing 7.5 shows some examples of this.

Short circuits will result if thorough gapping is not carried out. The rule is that there must be a gap between any power feed and any frog if the approach to the frog does not pass through the turn-out first. Instruction sheets which elaborate on the need for gapping are provided with most makes of live frog turn-out.

Sectionalising With isolating turn-outs sidings can be sectionalised merely by setting the turn-out against the siding. But there are many instances where it is convenient to hold a locomotive temporarily while others are run nearby. A classic example is the engine shed road – a loco comes off duty and runs up to the end of the road, then another runs up the same siding behind it. If all the track was live both locos would move as soon as the second loco was switched into the siding. However, if the end of the siding is itself isolated and switched out of the circuit any loco in that section will be held dead no matter what happens elsewhere in the same siding. An ordinary on/off switch (available from all the main track makers) can be wired in to do this, although most firms make isolating track sections which are ready wired.

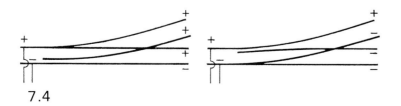

7.4

A similar arrangement can be made at the end of terminus roads, allowing the train engine to be uncoupled and left behind when a fresh loco is run on to the back of the train for the return journey.

This sectionalisation principle can be applied to whole segments of a larger layout where more than one controller may be used, or a single controller may be switched among sections as required. A typical arrangement is shown in drawing 7.7. A train can be run in whichever of the three sections is switched into the circuit, trains in the other sections being held dead.

Sectionalising is also needed on twin track layouts where 'up' and 'down' lines are in effect two different layouts each with trains running on them. Drawing 7.8 shows the basic principle.

Reverse Loops The other problem sometimes encountered is the reverse loop or the turning triangle, for here are track formations which turn the complete train and cause the tracks to double back on themselves. One way to overcome the problem is to avoid a layout which features either of these track formations. However, some 'out and back' track layouts are to be found where reverse loops are needed. The loop goes round and meets itself, and it will be apparent that the polarity clashes. Without gaps a short circuit would be caused. Therefore the loop itself can be treated as an isolated section while the train is in it. The control unit is switched in and out of this isolated section using what is called a 'double pole double throw' (DPDT) switch (made by several firms and easily obtained). Drawing 7.9 shows the principle for a reverse loop and drawing 7.10 a turning triangle.

When the train runs on to the loop the turn-out is changed for the return direction and the DPDT is made, which reverses the current in the main line, so that it matches that in the loop. The train then completes the circuit smoothly.

If this idea of wiring reverse loops is still baffling, then Fleischmann and Roco come to the rescue by producing complete reverse loop wiring outfits with all the necessary breaks done in two sections which are incorporated in the loop, and with the necessary wires and switches ready for installation.

Turn-out Control and Control Panels Mention of fitting point motors to turn-outs was made in the previous chapter. In all but the simplest power units the terminals for a 16 volt ac auxiliary output are clearly marked, and these provide the power source

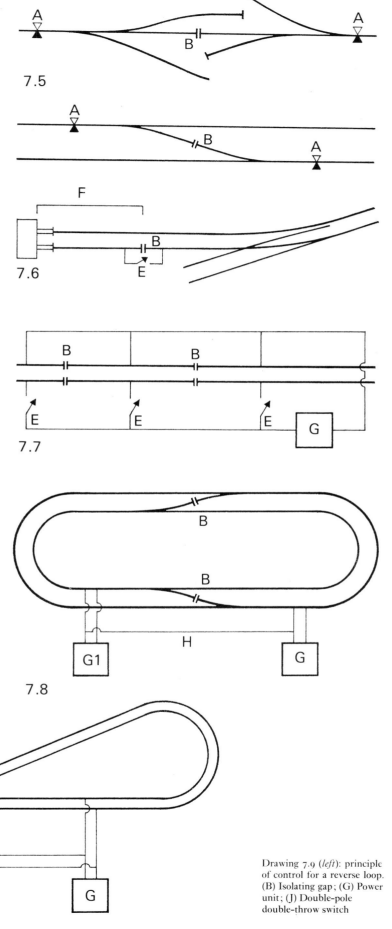

7.5

7.6

7.7

7.8

Drawing 7.9 (*left*): principle of control for a reverse loop. (B) Isolating gap; (G) Power unit; (J) Double-pole double-throw switch

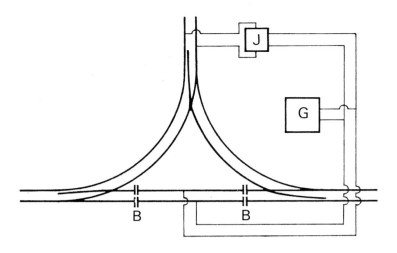

Drawing 7.10: principle of
control for a turning triangle.
(B) Isolating gap; (G) Power
unit; (J) Double-pole
double-throw switch

to be attached and switches to be mounted.

In making a control panel, a popular idea is to paint or mark a diagram of the track circuit on, say, a plywood panel, using two brass round-headed screws at each turn-out position (one each side of the marked track), attaching the leads to the point motor on the protruding screws at the back of the panel. ECM, Peco, Lima and others make an electric pencil probe. This is wired to the leads from the ac power supply. Touching the probe to the necessary screw head completes the circuit to actuate the point motor and throw the turn-out. This is a simple and effective method, particularly good where the track work is more complex and much turn-out operation is required. It is quick and fool-proof, and preferred by many to lever switches or push buttons.

Drawing 7.10: principle of control for a turning triangle. (B) Isolating gap; (G) Power unit; (J) Double-pole double-throw switch

to work the point motors and other accessories such as signals or uncoupling ramps. Switches must be included in the circuit. Hornby produce a good one (called a 'passing contact lever switch') but so do many other makers. The Hornby diagram (drawing 7.11) shows these switches in circuit with the ac output to control not only the turn-outs but also some related signals. The same diagram also shows the use of two power units (controllers), one to control each track of a double track layout, and two 'on/off lever switches' to control isolated sections of track as previously described. Hornby make their lever switches in different colours according to function and all can be banked together and their own control units include space for a track diagram

Drawing 7.11: wiring for traditional 12 volt dc control

What the Makers Offer All that has been described so far can be done by buying any suitable wire or switch gear from a hobby store and working things out. But the leading model train makers have made great efforts in recent years to make life easy: Hornby, Fleischmann, Atlas, Arnold, Minitrix, Roco, Lima, H & M and Peco are among the firms who have really got everything together in terms of equipment. Each offers a full range of switches and their catalogues explain how everything works and are related to requirements. Of the various makes Hornby and Fleischmann are probably the easiest for the absolute beginner to follow. Hornby have simple robust switches adequate for use on quite simple layouts which may have only a few remote

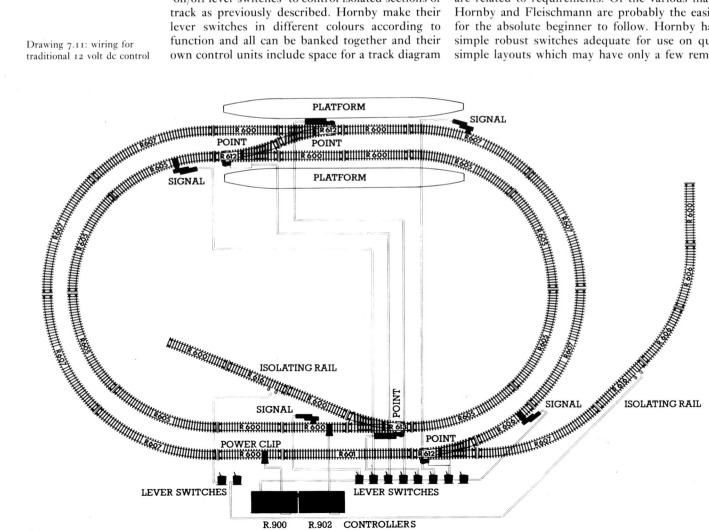

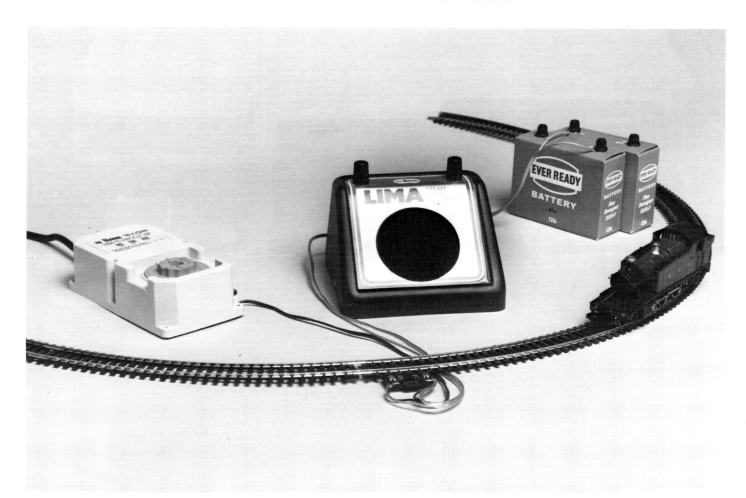

turn-outs and isolating sections, while Fleischmann have a system of great sophistication (it is also a little more expensive) which reproduces in miniature the block system as used in real railways. All the parts needed to make up a track diagram are also produced in plug-together form.

The other makers mentioned all have control equipment which comes somewhere between these two in style. It pays to get the catalogues of all or some of these firms and study the sections on control equipment. Further, one of the track plan books put out by these different makers can be followed for a layout plan, then wired just as the track diagram shows. This works remarkably well.

Sound Systems Another recent development is the production of simulated sound. The systems are many and varied and new ideas are coming along all the time. Firms in this field, such as Q Kits, offer small speakers which fit inside the loco or under the layout and are linked to the Q Kits power unit (which replaces the conventional unit in this case). Various effects buttons are fitted such as 'hiss', 'whistle', 'chuff' and the operator presses the buttons accordingly, the actual sound being linked to locomotive speed.

Bachmann have a good self-contained system in several of their locos, which gives good diesel or steam sound effects, again related to loco speed. For whistles or horns a battery-powered press-button unit is put into the track leads. There are yet others, and some firms like Lima offer a simple system with a track-side speaker which is synchronised with the power unit and can be added as an accessory later.

Command Control If this book had been written five or six years earlier the main sophistication to be covered by a chapter on wiring would be 'cab control', mentioned briefly earlier. This is a wiring and sectionalising system whereby a locomotive can be controlled from one power unit (ie, the cab) while passing through several electrically linked sections of a complex layout. It allows several trains to be run at a time on different parts of a layout, although not, of course, in the same section. The wiring for cab control is quite complicated, as are the requirements for switches and the control panel. Cab control needs several operators and is the system most commonly seen on large layouts.

In recent years, however, the new technology of 'command control' makes 'cab control' rather obsolate. The use of silicon chips and microprocessors means that a 'memory' can be put into what is, in effect, a computerised system, so that numerous locomotives can be run simultaneously on a larger layout without the wiring and switching complications associated with cab control. A modeller building a big layout (or intending to build one in the future) can take advantage of these recent developments to use command control rather than the old cab control.

Various systems have been produced, some compatible with others and some not. Hornby's Zero-1, H & M's M5000 system, Salota, and MTC are

Lima's sound simulator with speaker synchronised to the speed controller is one of several sound systems available

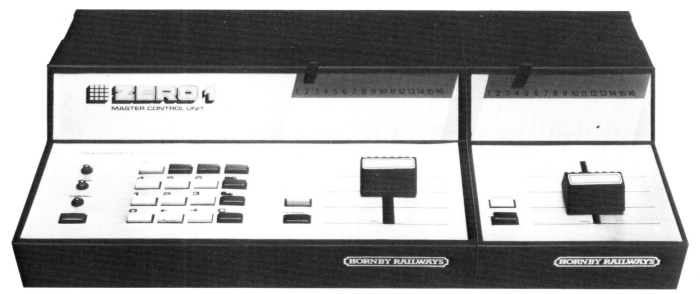

The master control unit with an attached 'slave' unit (*right*) of the Hornby Zero–1 system

The Compspeed Rambler by ECM is an excellent 'new generation' control system which gives very smooth operation and constant speed. Note the 'walk about' control box

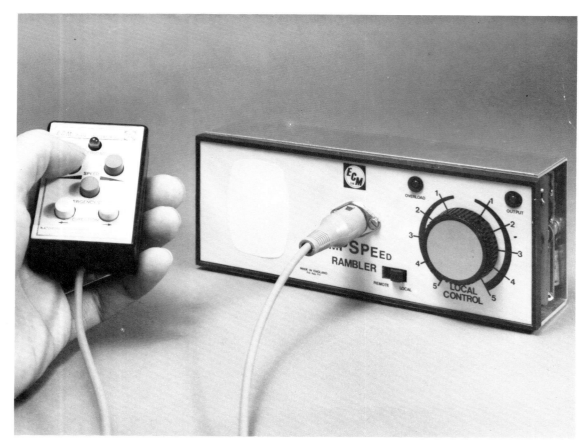

Opposite: old-time railroading in the United States. The classic HO scale 'American' 4–4–0 with 1880s period stock is enhanced with a wintry effect, using salt

among the systems available. ECM produce the Selectrol, a clever system which allows even non-adapted locos to be run with those specially adapted for command control.

There are differences between the command control system and the old conventional system. For a start they are in no way compatible with each other (except as noted with Selectrol). The old conventional 12 volt dc system depends on varying the actual motor speed in the loco by direct means and there is no other control apart from that. With command control a constant 20 volt ac current is fed into the circuit all the time. Then signals are relayed down the track from a master control board, cover-ing stop, start, direction, inertia, and so on. Each loco must be fitted with a 'memory' module, unique to a particular loco on the layout. The memory picks up signals and acts accordingly. The instructions are tapped out on a keyboard which quite closely re-sembles the standard keyboard of a pocket calculator, except that the functions are different. As the voltage system is different it is obvious that locos not fitted with the module will not work on a command control layout – and indeed they might be damaged. There-fore once a modeller decides to go for command control, total commitment is a prerequisite.

It is the module in the loco which changes the current to 12 volt dc. Hence every loco must first be

The German scene is well captured by David Armitage on his authentically detailed HO layout which uses ready-to-run locos and rolling stock to great effect. The signal box is adapted from a Vollmer kit

On this narrow ledge joining two layout sections there was no room for fully modelled scenery, but the large calendar illustration with a river bend in view gives impressive 'depth' and a convincing setting where the baseboard is only 4in wide. Locomotive is an ex-Prussian 2–6–2T in French Etat service from the Piko HO range. Note use of foam ballast inlay

fitted with a module before it can be used safely on the layout. Each module is coded differently. On a typical system (like Zero-1) it is possible to run up to 16 locos simultaneously and control up to 69 points and accessories. Basically the system plugs in on a 'two-wire' basis, although it gets slightly more complicated than that with some layouts. There is an accessory module with Zero-1 which really makes turn-out and signal control very easy. There are also slave controllers so that operators can be conveniently seated round the layout.

The Hornby diagram (drawing 7.12) shows the layout previously illustrated now wired for command control; the simplicity of the set-up is immediately evident by comparison with the previous identical track plan.

These command control systems were developed

for OO/HO but can be used for N (except Lima) if there is room to fit the module, or they can be used for O Gauge.

When properly installed command control is obviously a fine way to run a layout. But it is not all honey. Some makes of locomotive give trouble when it comes to fitting the module, while cleanliness and good maintenance are of prime importance because the system is more sensitive than conventional dc.

Installing a command control system is not entirely straightforward for anybody unfamiliar with electrics. However, there are new developments all the time in command control, and it is obviously the system which will dominate layout wiring and control in the future.

Märklin The name of Märklin does not appear

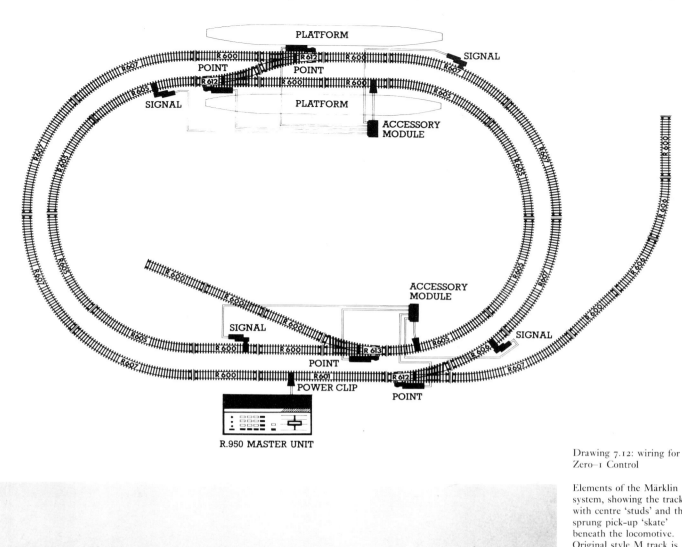

PLATFORM

SIGNAL

POINT   POINT

SIGNAL

PLATFORM

ACCESSORY
MODULE

R 607 R 600 R 612 R 600
R 612 R 600 R 601
R 605
R 607
R 605

ACCESSORY
MODULE

R 600
R 600
SIGNAL
R 601 R 600
R 605
SIGNAL
R 613
POINT
R 606
R 607
R 601
R 612
POINT

POWER CLIP

R.950 MASTER UNIT

Drawing 7.12: wiring for
Zero–1 Control

Elements of the Märklin
system, showing the track
with centre 'studs' and the
sprung pick-up 'skate'
beneath the locomotive.
Original style M track is
seen here

among the references to main commercial model
train makers so far in this chapter, because most of
their electrical systems differ from the conventional
12 volt dc system used by other manufacturers.

The Märklin Mini-Club Z Gauge system is 8 volt
dc rather than 12 volt dc, due to the very small size
of the motors. While there are several power units
suitable for use with Mini-Club locomotives (for
example the ECM Compspeed), great care should be
taken in selection, and to be on the safe side the very
good units specially produced by Märklin for Z
Gauge are best. The basic Z Gauge sets come with
one of these units in any case.

The Märklin HO and Gauge 1 systems work on
the original 16 volt ac power supply method dating
from the early days of electric model railways. Pick-
up used to be from a centre third rail, but Märklin
use a more sophisticated version of this, called stud
contact. The conductor strip is carried under the

sleepers with a stud pushed up almost invisibly
through each sleeper. A long sprung skate carried
under the loco chassis ensures reliable pick-up.
Although most modellers prefer the convenience of
two-rail dc electrification, the Märklin ac system has
some positive advantages. Reliable operation
through turn-outs, elimination of any polarity
worries on reversing loops and turning triangles,
and ease of sectionalising are among the merits of
the system.

The Märklin Gauge 1 system is two-rail but it is
still 16 volt ac. However, Märklin offer alternative dc
locos in this scale, while certain locomotive models
in the HO range are produced in two-rail dc form
under the Hamo name. Some specialist dealers also
offer a dc conversion service from standard Märklin
ac models.

What is outstanding about the Märklin system in
any scale is the thoroughness and simplicity of their

electrical engineering. A standardised colour coding is used for all wires, push buttons and sockets and every piece sold for electrical operation is complete with all wire and switches. Colour diagrams are provided and even a modeller with absolutely no knowledge at all of electrical circuits cannot go wrong if all the colours are matched. Quality is high and the equipment works well whatever the scale.

Overhead Supply Most new or modernised railway systems these days are electrically operated using overhead catenary for the power supply. This is reflected in the growing numbers of attractive electric locomotives which are appearing on the market in all scales.

Now it is true that adding the overhead catenary system with which to run these realistically involves some extra financial outlay and the work needed for installation. If either of these problems is daunting, stay with diesel or steam age traction, but there are great attractions in electric locos, vintage or modern, and many European railway systems are extensively electrified these days. Lima, Vollmer, Hadley/JV, Märklin, Berliner-Bahn, Piko and Sommerfeldt, all offer sets and components for making realistic catenary in OO/HO, TT (Berliner-Bahn only), Z (Märklin only), N (Vollmer and Sommerfeldt only), but supply is sometimes difficult.

What overhead supply does offer is the chance of an extra pick-up – from the wire – thus allowing an added element of flexibility, for another engine on the same track can pick-up from the rails in the normal way. Most overhead electric model locomotives have a simple switch which enables pick-up to be selected from the pantograph and the catenary or the track. However, in some model locos (and passenger equipment come to that) the pantograph is dummy and has no wiring to allow overhead pick-up.

For those who do not want to get involved in the extra power circuit involved in overhead current supply, then Arnold produce several electric locos and trains in N Gauge, and their overhead system is dummy. They make the catenary posts in plastic kit form – very neat and easy to assemble – and then sell a spool of thin rubberised 'wire' which is elastic. It is strung through the posts and maintains a realistic tension as the pantographs of the locos or trains pass under it. However, it is completely cosmetic and pick-up is through the track in the normal way. For OO/HO or TT the same idea could be adopted.

What is not in doubt is that electric locomotives and trams are very attractive to many modellers. Using one or other of the systems described here they can be run realistically. If one cares at all about good realism it will be a point of honour to string up overhead wiring before running trams and electric locomotives.

Trams also work from overhead supply, but the gantries are of lighter construction. Eric Slagg used knitting needles to make the posts on his fine Newtor tram layout

BRIDGE STREET JUNCTION

Scenery

In the early days of model railways only scant attention was paid to scenery and some layouts were never run on anything more than bare baseboards with, perhaps, just a station building and signal box as a gesture towards a realistic setting. All that has changed, of course, and the scenic setting today is every bit as important as the trains and track. Indeed, in an age where many modellers are all buying or building trains from the same manufacturers, so that popular models are commonplace, the scenery can be the vital part of a layout that gives it individuality and character.

After the technical skills and care required for baseboard building, track laying, and wiring, scenic work might seem very easy, or it might even be regarded as a soft option demanding less concentration than other aspects of the hobby. In fact, as the scenery completes the overall setting for everything else, it needs careful thought and work if it is to succeed.

As with everything else connected with the model railway hobby, the scenic side needs thought from the very beginning and should not be left until the tracks are laid. In other words, a layout should be conceived in total terms. Once a track plan is established (or even before it is finalised) the setting should be considered – the scenic side visualised. Many layouts get their setting because of the nostalgic connections of the owner.

A small layout in a confined space justifies sharp curves and short trains – a steep, rugged, hilly terrain provides the perfect excuse for the physical limitations of the railway line. Not surprisingly then many layouts feature quite steep hills, single line working and generally cramped surroundings and they are visually interesting because of it. By contrast railways in flatter areas tend to sprawl, and sometimes the scenery is monotonous too. For example a prairie setting can be deadly dull (and it can be in real life, too). On the other hand a steep Alpine setting well modelled looks both exciting and romantic.

Getting away from the inherently flat nature of the average new baseboard is therefore a worthwhile objective, and scenery can go above or below track level. Personal background research is most useful, and familiarity with the surroundings is an aid to visualising a layout in its finished setting. Obviously if an area can be visited (and photographed), then so much the better.

There are few, if any, fixed rules about building model scenery for the end result is what matters – just as it does in a painting. Thus there are numerous methods of making hills and hilly areas, and here we will look only at well-proven recent methods which are easy and effective. There is much more advice on aspects of scenic matters in the model railway magazines, and do always remember there *are* alternatives to all the methods described here.

Making the Basic Hills Land is undulating and even 'flat' areas are not as flat as model railway baseboards. So the first concern is getting hills in place. The quick and easy method is to collect junk expanded styrene foam, or buy cheap foam ceiling tiles which are a good substitute for chunks of expanded styrene foam. The illustrations in this chapter show the exact way of using expanded styrene blocks to make typical hills, mountains, and embankments.

These show that scrap expanded polystyrene packing is built up to the height required for the highest part of the hill. Flat pieces cut from ceiling tile with an old knife give some contoured formers which will form the slopes of the hill. Off-cuts piled on top of the hill give an irregular shape. Use white PVA glue and track pins or carpet tacks to hold all the plastic foam together. Use plenty of newspaper below the baseboard because scrap plastic foam will carry everywhere. Now cut ½ in (13mm) strips from old cereal or detergent packets and interlace them to form a cage over the expanded polystyrene formers. Use pins or adhesive tape to hold everything loosely together. This gives a good impression of the finished contours, even as a basic skeleton. An alternative to card strips is ordinary masking tape which can be criss-crossed over the formers even more quickly than you can interlace the card strips. However, masking-tape is rather more expensive than strips cut from old card packaging. In almost every case the framework built up will hold its shape, supported only by the contoured formers. If there should be any tendency to collapse or sag on the part of the card or masking tape cage, just push crumpled newspaper under the section to give it support. The last point to make about this substructure is that thick card, hardboard, or wood can be used instead of ceiling tiles or styrene sheet to make the contoured formers.

If there are to be rocky outcrops or cliff faces, use expanded styrene sheet cut roughly to shape. Several layers can be canted or placed horizontally with slight displacement between them to give the effect of rock strata.

Low embankments or cuttings, particularly at the baseboard edge or along the back of the baseboard, can often be carved roughly to shape from solid blocks of expanded styrene using an old knife. When

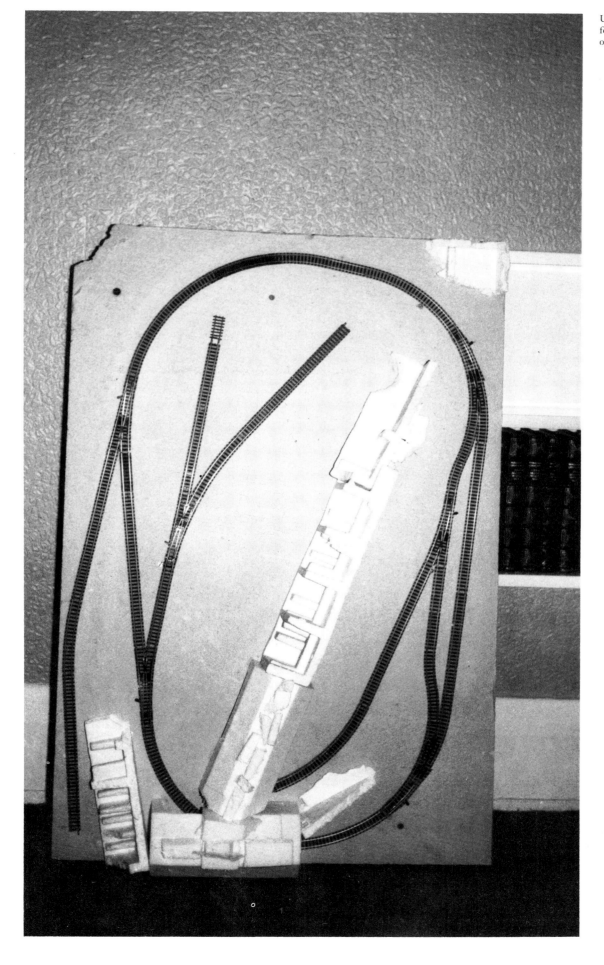

Use scrap expanded styrene
foam to make up the core or
outline of hills or cuttings

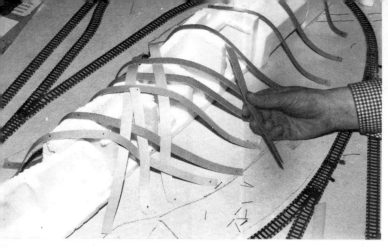

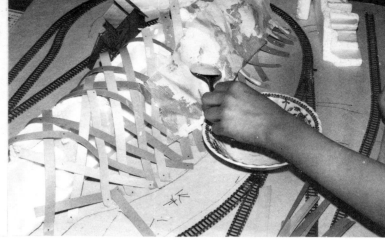

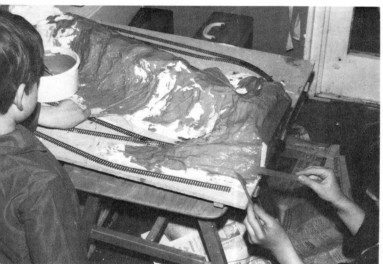

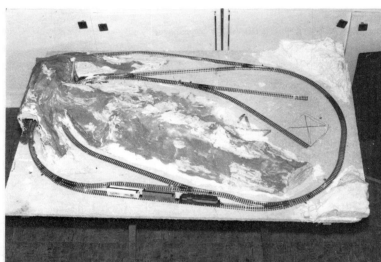

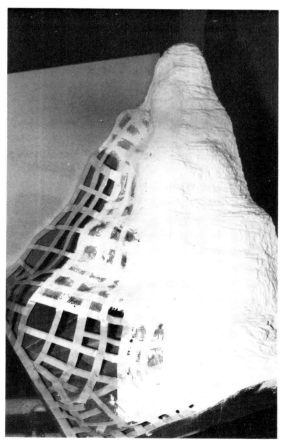

Top, left: make a 'cage' by interlacing strips of card cut from old cereal packets or similar scrap card. Note outline of hills marked out on board and the pins used to hold down the ends of the strips

Top, right: place strips of tarlton (or similar gauze-like material) over the card strips and use a thin mix of modelling compound to hold them in place

Above, left: use a second coat of thicker modelling compound (coloured with powder paints if desired) over the first thin covering after a 24 hour drying period.

Above, right: the hill is now completed, although it is yet to be grassed and afforested

Right: the 'hard shell' technique for making a 4ft high 'mountain', sectioned from left to right to show the stages of construction

cut quickly through or broken, the rough edges which result will often give quite a good rock or cliff effect, even before they are given any scenic treatment. Low hills can be made by glueing several ceiling tiles one above the other and carving the lot roughly to shape to fit the site.

Now stand back and look at the bare structural work. Check it does not come close enough to the track to encroach on it, or worse still to foul passing trains. With no trains on the track clearances may look generous, but run a long coach round a curve and you may find the corner of a buffer beam hits the cutting side. Avoid such mistakes by running trains of longer locos and vehicles round the track at this sub-structure stage. If necessary (or even if only in doubt) cut back cuttings or hills to make sure nothing will be hit by a passing train.

Now the messier work begins. First cover every inch of carefully laid and tested track with strips of newspaper. Use track pins and masking tape to hold all the paper strips securely in place. This is a vital step which must not be overlooked, for it will prevent paint, plaster and the like from dropping on the running rails and spoiling the electrical integrity.

There are several types of plaster suitable for forming the actual scenic surface. Foremost is Artex, a powder type of compound made by British Gypsum Ltd and available from them, and also sold specially packaged for scenic work by Jack Kine Models. The American equivalent to this is called

An alternative method of
making hills, using chicken
wire, paper, and plaster over
wood contour formers,
demonstrated on the Chiltern
Green N Gauge layout of
The Model Railway Club

Hydrocal, then there is an almost identical material in the Faller range, called Hydrozell. If these are not obtainable, ordinary patching plaster of the Polyfilla type may be used, although it is heavier and more brittle than Artex. Also needed is a quantity of light material, to hold the scenic surface compound. The ideal material is buckram or tarleton which is a stiff gauzelike cloth used for stiffening dresses, available cheaply from haberdashers. But old bandages, gauze, hessian, net curtaining or similar material can be used.

Cut the material into convenient strips – say 3in × 4in or 3in × 5in (75mm × 100mm or 75mm × 125mm) and start laying these strips loosely over the cage structure with pins or adhesive tape to hold the first few pieces in place. Make each piece overlap the next. They will then hold each other in place long enough for one to move on to the next stage. Mix the Artex or other compound with water to the consistency of thick soup. Get a stiff domestic size paint brush, and quickly paint the thin mix of compound over the gauze strips with particular care to cover all overlaps thoroughly. Do not worry if the stuff runs, for the track is covered over with paper (remember?). If any gaps open up in the gauze strips, place another strip of gauze over the hole and dab more compound over it. When everything is covered leave the whole lot overnight to dry thoroughly. On a very small layout – 6ft × 4ft (1·85m × 1·20m) or smaller – it may be possible to do all this work in a single

session (in a layout in modular or sectional form, then each section makes a convenient working unit).

Next day mix more compound, this time to the consistency of double cream – in other words more powder less water. At this stage brown or black powder colour can be added to 'kill' the white of the compound – if done carefully this should give a realistic earth colour which will obviate some painting work later on.

Now go over the entire scenic area again, this time painting the thicker material all over the thin 'shell' which was formed by the original coating and filling any odd imperfections or dimples. Use kitchen paper towels dipped in the compound to amend or alter any imperfections. Smooth this surface off if required for grass and work on any bare rock faces to give a realistic surface. For such effects as scree or gravel surfaces stipple the compound as it dries with a scriber or the bristles of a stiff paint brush. A palette knife, old ice lolly stick, or old screwdriver can be used to work the surface of the compound to smooth it off. Keep a pot of water handy to clean off brushes and scribers to prevent them getting clogged.

Where there is expanded styrene left exposed, as for cliff faces or complete rock cuttings, just apply the same thin layer of compound to the bare styrene. In this case cover all the styrene, even the non-visible parts which might, for instance, be at the back edges of the baseboard. The compound makes

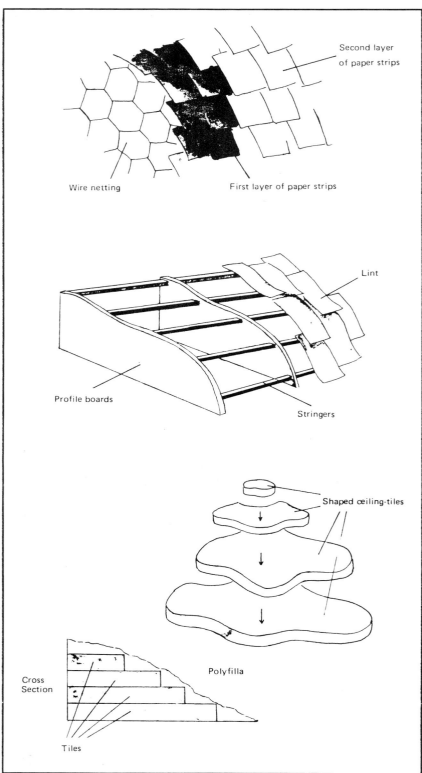

Second layer
of paper strips

Wire netting

First layer of paper strips

Lint

Profile boards

Stringers

Shaped ceiling-tiles

Polyfilla

Cross
Section

Tiles

Drawing 8.1: common alternatives to the 'hard shell' method of hill making. *Top:* chicken wire, paper, and plaster. *Centre:* contour or profile boards, wood stringers and paper, but here showing a further alternative for smooth grassland – surgical lint dyed green. *Bottom:* ceiling tiles cut to shape, layered, and plastered over

the styrene foam structure very tough and rigid. While the compound is setting, etch in strata lines and other features on exposed rock face sections as required. If the first attempt is not 'right', it can be smoothed over and corrected while the compound is still wet. Obviously there is a degree of skill involved in getting a convincing looking terrain and the study of actual geological features or books on the subject is commended. Hills which are too steep are a common fault, but when making scenery in a confined space bear in mind that one can take liberties.

A hill *can* be made steeper than it would be in real life if it is covered with plenty of trees to conceal the angle of the slope, or in rocky and mountainous terrain the cliffs and bluffs can be brought much closer together and closer to the railway tracks than they might be in real life, so long as the clearances for the trains are not affected.

With all the hills and contoured areas covered, areas like roads and level crossings might need just a thin layer of the ground mix compound painted over them to give texture. If a level crossing from a kit or accessory pack is used, plaster can be taken over the edges to merge it in to the adjoining roadway so that it no longer looks like a separate item standing on a flat surface. Similarly, if there are key structures standing on plastic bases, bring the compound over the edges to merge the bases nicely into the surrounding countryside. Nothing will destroy realism more than a free-standing base perched above the ground area.

Other Scenic Methods The method of making hills described here gives light hollow shell scenery, adding virtually nothing to the weight of the layout. An older more traditional method of making hills involved using hardboard, plywood, chipboard, or other wood cut to the hill shapes and the contoured formers with strips of battening and/or chicken wire or brown paper as the basic covering. This is packed out with crumpled newspaper or even old wood offcuts. The whole is covered with patching plaster of the Polyfilla type, then given textured ground treatment as before.

Yet another much used method is Mod-Roc or other plaster impregnated bandages. These are sold as packs and the frame is built up as before with the plaster bandages applied in strips over the top and smoothed to shape as required. This saves the need to mix plaster compound.

Surface Texturing After the ground surface has set hard it can be textured and afforested. There are several ways of doing this, as the illustrations show. Ground covering materials are sold in virtually all model shops (Woodland Scenics, Branch Out, Jack Kine, Dee Ess, Noch, Faller and Riko are among many brand names to look for). Some are rather coarse and the modern more finely ground types of 'scatter' are to be preferred. At its simplest, a grass surface can be made by painting the area to be covered a suitable grass green, using poster paint, acrylics, household emulsion, or ordinary matt modelling colours. Then the painted area is painted over with ordinary office paste and the scatter material shaken over it. Any excess can be tipped off (by tilting the layout board over newspaper) after work has set. An alternative is to scatter the grass over the dry surface, use an atomiser spray to cover it with a wetting agent (water with a drop of liquid detergent), then drop over it watered down acrylic matt medium varnish or diluted PVA glue (this runs through the wetting agent and sets transparent to hold all the scatter material in place). The technique is the same as is used for 'bonded ballasting' previously described. It can be used, too, for holding down scattered scree or coal so that it looks to be loose but is firmly glued to the baseboard surface.

Getting away from these basic methods of adding surface texture there are some newer ideas. The German firm of Noch specialises in scenic material, including Struegrass, in a puff container. It is puffed out over a glued surface but as the particles of scatter material carry an electrostatic charge the particles stand on end giving the most realistic effect of long growing grass. Noch also make aerosol sprays of various types of grass (meadow, mountain, marsh, etc) which are squirted over the surface rather as hair lacquer is applied. The texture is realistic and the process swift – a good time saver. All areas *not* to be grassed must be masked off with paper and avoid piling up a thick layer (in other words keep the spray moving) for if the glue in the compound gets too thick it may be affected by light and discolour in patches. Mud is included in the same range. Naturally these more sophisticated materials are more expensive than cheap bags of 'scatter' but they are quick and look good, if only used sparingly in the foreground.

Yet another technique is the American 'zip texturing'. This uses powder paints (or powder dyes) to give grass, rock and earth effects. Here the surface is painted, or it is brushed over with water if already painted, and the coloured powders are shaken over the surface through a strainer again so that they adhere in powder form to the wet surface which then dries and holds them.

Afforestation Trees offer no problems to the modeller today. There are quite cheap ready-made fir trees readily available in hobby shops, under brand names such as Vero, Heki, Noch, and Jordan. These do tend to look like Christmas cake decorations if used as supplied, and a way to make them look much more realistic is to coat them with white PVA glue, then roll them in scatter material which has been sprinkled in a shallow cardboard lid, and leave to dry. Riko, Piper, Vero, Noch, Faller and others offer ready-made trees in abundance, covering all well known species, while Britains have a range of plastic plug-together trees. These, and other plastic trees, tend to have a shiny look which can be overcome either by painting with matt clear varnish or adding scatter material.

Woodland Scenics, and others of a similar type, are actually kits containing realistic cast metal trunks, which may be bent to varied shapes, and separate foliage which is glued to the trunks. They are extremely pleasing models of actual species, although the soft metal of the trunks can make them vulnerable.

Trees can be made very cheaply. One method is to bend wire or wire flex into a trunk shape, coat it with modelling plaster to give the bark texture then add foliage. Good twigs which are clean and dry, picked up in garden and park, can also be used with added foliage – choose the size of twig to suit a scale. Twigs without foliage can be cut to size for tree trunks, tree stumps, or dead trees. A way of making pine trees is to tease out green garden twine into strands, catch clumps between two wires then twist the wires by gripping them in a hand drill to catch

This sequence shows the exact procedure for making realistic bushes and scrub from rubberised horsehair and scatter material. It is suitable for any scale

the strands and give a tall pine tree shape.

Bushes of the gorse, scrub, or hazel variety are most realistically made from rubberised horse hair (used in some upholstery work). This can be purchased specifically for modelling (as in the Jack Kine Hedging kit). It is cut and teased to size (long strips if used for hedging). Dab white PVA glue over each piece and dip in scatter material. This adheres to give the effect of fine branches with leaves. Small pieces of rubberised horse hair can also be used to make the foliage for trees, sticking each piece to the wire stem or twig used for the trunk.

If ready-made trees are used extensively, it is advisable to twist them a little or add extra foliage to make them look a little different from the standard item. Trees are 'planted' simply by drilling a hole in the scenery and glueing them in with a dab of white PVA. Make sure they are straight and watch the grouping.

Water Representation Lakes, ponds, rivers, harbours, and puddles, often cause problems in representation, and again there are no firm rules. One of the oldest methods is still the easiest and is surprisingly effective for rivers and harbours. Simply make the river bed as flat wood, card or softboard, flush at water level, paint it to depict water – blues, greens, browns, even flecks of white – then screw up cling film or Cellophane, open it out, cut to shape, spread over the painted surface, and

Realistic water made by painting layers of clear varnish over a wood 'river bed'

secure it with a few dabs of white PVA glue or varnish at the edges. Any driftwood, piers, buoys, or waterline boats, can be placed on top of it afterwards. It is so simple that many modellers nowadays forget about it.

For very still water, as in ponds, lakes or enclosed harbours, a sheet of acetate or clear plastic can be used. Here it is possible to model the bottom, complete with weeds and old junk, paint it, and then fit the clear sheet at water level. If necessary a ledge can be made to hold the sheet when plastering the depression which is to depict the lake or pond. This system gives 'depth' and some realistic reflections. Acetate may be rippled a little by painting cellulose (eg nail varnish) over it, but experiment first on a piece of scrap. If in doubt be content with clear still 'water'. Weed and seaweed can be depicted with scatter material of suitable texture and colour.

'Water glass' used in handicrafts is another handy and realistic method of depicting water. It is mixed and poured like stiff water and sets solid. It is messy, however, and the areas to be covered must be perfectly horizontal or there will be sloping water! Also the ends of the baseboard or area must be dammed to stop the liquid running away when poured. Ripple glass is an alternative to this.

Waterfalls or flowing streams can be represented by pouring many layers of clear gloss varnish along the course, layer after layer over a period of time, and for bigger waterfalls it is best to resort to Cellophane or cling film again. Use about six layers, curling and glueing the bottom edges and making vertical streaks with white paint on each layer before affixing the next. Dribbles or drainage water running from pipes, as in harbour walls or under embankments, can be depicted most effectively by twisting lengths of clear adhesive tape and glueing them into the pipe end. For surface water, in say meadow or marsh, clear varnish or even clear office paste may be used, simply painted into the depressions where the surface water is supposed to lay.

Scenic Backgrounds Backscenes are widely sold in hobby shops and all are good, although they are over-familiar because so many modellers buy them and use them. For something different old country calendars can be cut out and used with the commercial backscenes, on a 'mix and match' basis with overlays to come up with something more exclusive in your layout.

Ripple glass used to depict a lake on Ross Pochin's famous Furness Railway EM Gauge layout. Note also painted backscene matched neatly to the foreground hills – the join is less obvious from a more normal viewing angle

Use hardboard cut to shape, or ⅛in (3mm) balsa sheet for TT, N, or Z, and paste on the backscenes, using a roller or milk bottle to ensure everything is flat and free of air bubbles. Leave to dry under a heavy weight (eg, a pile of books) so that the board does not curl or warp while the glue dries.

Backscenes can be used in long lengths if needs be – say on a narrow shelf layout. Better still, use short sections to fill in gaps – as between two actual modelled hills. A great illusion of depth is created. Disguise the join by making a hill or bank crest which rises higher than the lower edge of the backscene, with bushes, buildings or trees to disguise vertical joins. Typical uses of backscenes are seen in several illustrations in this book.

Care is needed with backscenes, largely because scale and perspective are awkward to achieve convincingly. Therefore, if collecting or even drawing illustrations for backscene use avoid scenes with sharp angles, or angles slightly above the horizontal, or illustrations where shadows are heavy or noticeable. Simple backscenes can be drawn and painted to suit the site. With all backscene work try to go for fairly subdued colours. For example, if the grass on a printed backscene is brighter than the scatter material used on the built-up scenery in front of it any illusion of depth will be lost. Blueish or hazy backgrounds are recommended.

Use of a backscene to depict an entire town. All the buildings are cut from catalogues and calendars and stuck as overlays on to an ordinary Peco countryside printed background. Note that even some figures of suitable size are included as they happened to be in the pictures selected. Essential requirement is to keep all such cut-outs strictly to scale size. A telegraph pole is being inserted here

Glue backscene sheets on to wood or hardboard backing, ensuring there are no air bubbles by using a roller, milk bottle, or rolling pin to get everything perfectly flat

Structures

Buildings are as integral a part of a model railway layout as the scenery. In many ways, indeed, buildings and structures can be used even more than the scenery to emphasise the nature of a layout and, conversely, it is essential that the buildings be in character with the setting. For example, if a layout is set firmly in the steam age, a modern square office block with large windows would be completely inappropriate. On the other hand, a red brick 1930s style block would be just the thing to add verisimilitude to the steam trains themselves. Similarly, if a layout depicts a rural branch line, a small Victorian station building would convey the correct atmosphere more surely than one of the 'pre-fab' station desgins of more recent times. Stone buildings will convey the impression of Normandy for a layout based in NW France, or South Devon for a GWR layout, but will not look particularly convincing if the trains are American, where wood or false front buildings would be more in keeping with the theme.

Providing model buildings and structures for a layout is no problem – there are literally hundreds of kits and components, with OO/HO and N scales best catered for. The kits range from simple and inexpensive card buildings to plastic or wood of the greatest sophistication. For example, it is possible to buy a complete replica of Bonn station which is about 9ft (2·74m) long in HO scale, while in the same scale there is a tiny halt only about $7\frac{1}{2}$ in (190mm) long but nonetheless an accurate replica of an original. Card models range from exquisitely printed replicas down to simple die-cut pop-together structures which can be assembled in minutes.

In the days before kits existed, structures had to be scratch-built from card or wood, but plastic card and pre-coloured card including embossed brick,

Paul King's fine model of a seafront cliff railway station is made from plastic card. Lettering on roof is from Slaters and the fencing by Ratio. Note realistic 'sag' built into roof and the cracks and discolouring in the stucco walls

The low relief building principle is well shown with this scratch-built model of a Georgian hotel in 4mm scale – the front only is fully modelled, as on a film set

stone, and tile sheets, makes scratch work even easier these days. Firms like Grandt Line make superb doors and windows in every imaginable style for use in scratch-building while others offer chimney pots and other accessories. Printed brick papers are also produced and are widely sold. Kit manufacturers like Faller also offer packs of useful spare items which can be used by scratch-builders. Scale drawings of buildings appear frequently in the model press.

It must be said, however, that the modern modeller can fill a layout with realistic structures without once having to get involved in scratch-building, for there are kits available to suit many needs; so many card kits and plastic kits are so readily available and so straightforward to construct that there is really no need (and no excuse) for a layout devoid of buildings. Indeed, the key buildings can be in place almost as soon as the track is down – a beginner wanting something quickly to give atmosphere can get hold of the simpler die-cut card kits like Builder Plus, Superquick, or Pop-a-Town. More sophisticated card kits, such as Bilteezi, Prototype, Diorama and so on require cutting out first, with much more detail work. Look in art shops and handicraft shops, too, for there are ranges of card

kits in various scales (and some wood kits) which are suitable for model railway use although not sold as such – for example, doll's house cut-outs and brick sheets which are useful for Gauge 1 and LGB scale. One tip if using printed brick or stone paper is to place the sheet over a piece of sandpaper and rub it hard. The texture of the sandpaper is transferred to the printed sheet to enhance its realism.

Card models are exceedingly useful in several ways. They are cheap and easy to build, but they are also very adaptable. Thus it is possible to 'cross-kit' by switching parts of buildings, and items like out-houses can be added by a little scratch-building. With card cut-outs one can play around to use only fronts and backs to give 'low relief' structures, ie, buildings with only the front inch or so actually modelled, so saving valuable inches of depth on narrow baseboards. It is also possible to cut out discarded segments from card kits to use as scenic 'flats' pasted on to the backscene. Judicious use of such flats behind fully modelled structures but in front of a scenic background can create the illusion of a crowded town in virtually no depth.

The range of plastic kits is immense, although the

Superb scratch-building by Dave Rowe on his famous Under Milkwood Welsh narrow gauge layout. Structures are built in blocks to match the road and capture the Welsh style to perfection

Conversion from card kits. The office is from a Bilteezi factory, the warehouse section from a 4mm scale Builder Plus garage, and the loading bank is from wood and card covered with building papers. The end result is an original-looking warehouse for TT Gauge

emphasis tends to be on the Germanic style of architecture because the biggest ranges of building kits come from Denmark (Heljan) and Germany/Austria (Faller, Pola, Vollmer, Kibri, Vero and others). Figures and road vehicles are abundant from the same countries and the standards are high (Preiser, Noch, Wiking, Herpa and Brekina are among the brand names). Even these European makers produce kits of buildings for other countries, however, and a reasonable selection of kits depicting (or adaptable to) British and American styles are included in the Danish and German ranges.

All these kits produced in Europe are pre-coloured so that after assembly they are ready for use. The colours tend to be a little bright, however, and the models can be improved with some toning down. Many can be fitted with interior lighting units which are available as accessories. There are also exterior lighting accessories available which allow such refinements as 'neon' signs for cinemas and flashing advertising hoardings as well as street accessories which light up. All scales are covered by these European makers, from LGB down to Z, although the O scale models are few and Märklin make some Gauge 1 size kits for their own trains in this scale.

In Britain there are well-known plastic kits by Airfix, Peco, Hornby, Wills and Merit, covering between them most requirements. For the American market there are kits by Life-Like, Bachmann, Atlas, Revell and others, all covering American style buildings. Several German Pola kits

are of American prototype as well. Almost unique to the American market, are wood kits of intricate detail which make into impressive models (Campbell is the leading name but there are others). These are available through specialist retailers outside the United States as are other American prototype kits.

The big problem with all these good things is their very wide availability, in that it leads to identical models appearing on layout after layout – the familiarity of many enthusiasts with the same old footbridges and engine sheds and other structures leads to a degree of cynicism on occasion! The key to success is to adapt the readily available kits to give them a degree of individuality and originality – in many cases only the most minor changes are needed.

Cross-kitting or part scratch-building are rich areas of exploration when it comes to making an original building. For example, an imposing factory may be made from combining two or three different kits. A classic old time warehouse may be made by combining three Airfix booking offices, one above the other, omitting the canopies and extensions and making card entrances over the original booking hall entrances with beams and hoists in the usual warehouse style. Several of the Bilteezi card cut-out structures are actually designed to be fitted together in various ways to make other buildings. The factory in this range can be altered to a dairy, and the schoolhouse or forge are designed so that they may be made in several ways – country shops or narrow gauge engine shed.

Quickest way to add grass is to use the Noch aerosol, literally a few seconds work

A simple way of making a tree, using a real twig and spare foliage from Woodland Scenics or other sources, glued to the branches of the twig

Cheap fir trees sold in all model shops can be enhanced by smearing them in PVA glue and rolling them in scatter material

To position trees, drill holes in the surface, add a blob of PVA glue and pop them in place. Use scatter material on the wet glue at the base to simulate grass. Texture of the rough moorland surface is a mix of scatter material and Streugras

This corner of the Willow Valley Railway shows a variety of trees used to disguise the steeper-than-real-life slope of the hill. Note also the ballasted and weathered sectional track, and the plaster carried over the back of the expanded styrene embankment (lower right). More trees are yet to be added

The Willow Valley Railway's 'workhorse', a Baldwin S–12 diesel supposedly leased from the Southern Pacific company whose colours it bears. This Athearn HO model has flywheel drive. Scenery is from expanded styrene blocks carved to shape, painted, and textured

The simplest way with scenery. Here Artex plaster compound mixed with powder colour to give a soil colour (sandy in this case) is applied by brush over an embankment made from layers of ceiling tiles

Making a level crossing – the first stage. Check flange clearance by running a vehicle through before glueing the centre section in place

Making a level crossing from balsa sheet. The approach ramps have been plastered over and wheel marks are being made in the 'mud' while the plaster is still wet

Small areas, such as roadside verges, are added last of all

Preceding pages: modern ready-to-run models of rolling stock and locomotives, such as these by Airfix/GMR, make it easy for even a beginner to create a simple layout like this. Most of the trees shown are from kits

Painting in rocky outcrops which are simply broken pieces of expanded styrene packing

Rock cutting made by breaking up expanded styrene packing blocks and leaving the broken faces exposed. Note also ballasted track and texturing which is a mix of powder paint sprinkled over paint, scatter material and Streugras

A favourite way of achieving an original appearance is partial scratch-building. Collect old powder tins, film tins, cigar tubes, card tubes, ball pens, and the like for they may be fashioned into all sorts of extras like gas holders, oil tanks, silos and water tanks. Scratch-building a new roof from card with individually cut tiles will make a kit-built structure look very different, particularly if some 'sag' is introduced into the roof ridge. Adding drain pipes, omitting barge boards, altering doors and window frames, adding curtains and/or window glazing, and many other dodges will change the

The Builder Plus factory effectively converted to a bigger factory in low relief by using all the walls on one side only. Model by Michael Andress

On the Midland layout of Sid Stubbs actual Midland Railway architecture is

reproduced, all scratch-built. Note also close-coupled MR four-wheel coaches and the grassy bank in front which is covered in dyed surgical lint

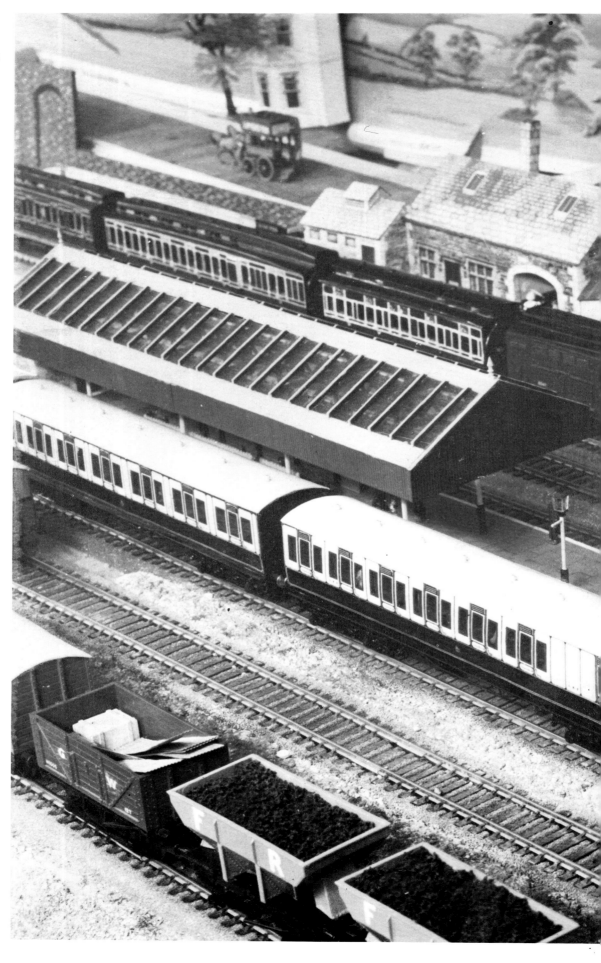

Excellent combination of Bilteezi card cut-outs and Airfix plastic platform canopies give an original look to this Edwardian period Furness Railway layout

appearance of standard kit-built structures. Sawing them in half to make low relief fronts only will also change the look of many structures. Combining two such halves will make a longer low relief structure. The possibilities are endless and really call for nothing more than some thought and study, relating the model to its position and function on a layout.

Grouping of buildings is another matter to which thought and consideration should be given. Try some groupings and alternative positions first. There is a tendency for buildings to be crammed on to every available space just for the sake of having a town near a station. But bear in mind that stations may be away from the crowded 'downtown' area so even a large station does not necessarily have to be hemmed in by other structures. As with other areas of the hobby it is better to have fewer well made and convincing models than a lot of indifferent and unrealistic ones. Like an artist, a layout builder is giving an impression of a landscape. In most layouts, and certainly all small ones, the landscape amounts only to the area near or around the railway tracks so there is no need to cram in buildings (or indeed scenic features) if they can just as easily be assumed to be 'off stage'. A siding serving a brewery does not necessarily mean that an entire brewery which might cover several acres in real life has to be modelled. The warehouse area which the siding actually abuts can be modelled and the rest of the brewery considered to be off the edge of the baseboard or it is made as a 'flat' behind the modelled area which might, itself, be only a low relief section.

Naturally small structures can be modelled in full, but never be averse to arranging a building in such a way as to suggest it is bigger or better than it really is. Using plenty of trees is a good way of disguising a small building. If it is partially masked by trees the small size or short length of a building may not be so noticeable.

Trying the positioning first is important. A single ramshackle hut in a small goods yard might look better than a very large goods shed. A station building may look better towards one end of a platform than right in the centre. All raised platforms have the effect of making any space look even shorter. This is one advantage of French, German and American country stations, since they generally have ground level platforms of no great length. In OO Gauge, however, a small British station with room for a three-coach train is over 3ft (0·9m) long, and this would be considered a very short length in real life. Therefore this platform should be made to look even longer; do this by making it as low as possible.

There are several other tricks like this. For example high buildings of, say, three stories, look bigger than they really are even if the actual ground area covered is actually very tiny. This is why grain elevators and oil tanks are good lineside facilities – even a very small grain elevator or silo makes a layout look like a busy operation. A small factory with a saw-tooth roof will by the same token look rather bigger and more impressive than the same size structure with a single bay roof, and anything

Improving a plastic kit structure. Jack Chipperfield ran white paint all over the lower storey of this Kibri German station, then wiped it off again to leave just the cement coursing between the bricks. Upper storey and roof are as yet untouched and still show as bright shiny plastic that needs toning down

A fine scratch-built signal box, detailed inside and out, adds distinction to the layout of Ken Thomas. This is 4mm scale

that straddles the track, like an ore tippler or a signal box on a gantry, or even a humble engine hoist, will again give an illusion of size.

The achievement of believable scenery and structures requires an artistic touch. Observation of the real thing helps: notice how trees are grouped, how walls sometimes partly tumble down, how gates sag on their hinges, how the grass is worn away near gates, how chimney pots are not always neat and regular, and how roof slates may be discoloured, not to mention walls. Paintwork fades and colours in buildings are rarely bright, so tone down all painting on building models by adding a touch of white to dark colours and a touch of black to light colours. Run watery acrylic white/grey over plastic moulded brickwork, then rub it off the surface before it dries. The paint will remain in the coursing between the bricks to enhance the realism. Do the same with black or grey paint on roofs, so that some paint lodges under the edges of slates. Put in some watery 'runs' near drainpipes. On plastic buildings leave the occasional door or window open rather than glue it firmly into its aperture.

If anything aim to understate everything. If one building suggests habitation, avoid the temptation to crowd in others into a tight space. Make sure all bases and bottom edges are covered so that the building looks bedded in. Failure to do this is a common scenic error.

Figures and accessories like bicycles, trucks, cars, and freight all need careful attention too. Make car windscreens dirty (leaving a swept arc for the wipers), show some dirt on tyres, add licence plates, and tone down bright plated parts. Check, even, that all the figures and vehicles are to correct scale. Some modern die-cast cars are, in fact, rather larger than OO/HO and this tends to become only too obvious when scale figures are placed nearby. Get rid of mould lines and flash on figures – shave them off – and also get rid of heavy bases. Either glue a tiny patch of clear plastic sheet on the feet or use Blue-Tak (or similar) smeared lightly under the feet to make the figure stand up without a base. Underpopulate rather than overpopulate. It is quite common to see model stations crammed with passengers when only one or two would capture the atmosphere. Make sure all figures are really upright and realistically grouped (observation again).

With both scenery and structures one can always return later to upgrade or replace areas or models.

Motive power

Today's railway modeller enjoys a rich selection of top quality model locomotives at very reasonable prices, with a choice and standard of excellence which just did not exist even ten years ago. For in the last few years new companies have entered the market and the struggle to capture a worthwhile segment of sales has led to a general upgrading of standards of finish and detailing. Hence recent models of British locomotives have the sort of detail (such as brake shoes, sand boxes, and separate hand rails) as were formerly found only on the leading European makes. Some of the 'last generation' models remain on sale. Most of these remarks apply to the popular scales of N and OO/HO where the available ranges of models are large, but even the larger scale modeller can rework the few ready-to-run models available.

A key to a good and successful model railway layout, efficient and realistic motive power, is yours almost without effort. Indeed, only spending money will limit the choice. A complete beginner might not know suffcent about the prototype locomotive to know whether a replica is very accurate, but in passing it is worth mentioning that the various model railway magazines generally review new releases when they appear. There are several key factors to consider, among them: (a) a beginner may want one of the cheaper, simpler 'train set' locomotives; (b) a particular favourite may only be available as one of the older generation of models which falls below modern standards of detail; (c) the current generation of models are highly detailed and of true scale appearance in virtually all respects; (d) modern models – and there are a few – which have

Recent ready-to-run models reach a high standard. The excellent Hornby 'Shire' class 4-4-0 of the LNER in OO Gauge includes smoke as an attractive extra feature

Conversion of the Airfix 1400 class loco to 5800 class as described in the text. Work entails removal of top feed and auto gear, adding new fittings (such as altered toolbox), renumbering, and addition of grime. Note wheels and motion blackened

minor errors of detail or dimension which need correction, and where even the best efforts of the designers have failed to ensure 100 per cent accuracy (there are instances where slight inaccuracy would be accepted in a 'favourite' loco).

Whatever the position, one certain thing is that pleasure can be derived from adding detail and/or individuality. In essence, what has now become known as the 'ready-to-run' locomotive model gives an excellent replica, looking most realistic and extremely well made – put it on the track and it will usually perform well straightaway. Lots of model railway enthusiasts do just that, and aside from the commended maintenance (oiling, brush replacement, and so on) they do not think of changing what the model manufacturer supplies. Indeed, this seems to be such a common attitude that even the models on many a big exhibition layout look just as though they are straight from the pages of the model manufacturer's catalogue – shiny, sparkling, and carrying the same running number as everybody else's model!

Why not try and do something about this? In the old days, modellers got some individuality into their

Improving the breed – 1. At left is a Lima 'Western' diesel as purchased; at right is the same model with detail fittings installed from an Adpakes accessory kit

layouts because nearly all locos had to be scratch-built or assembled from kits. Today many more modellers can join in the model railway hobby simply because so much is available in the 'ready-to-run' category, but essentially one important element of the model railway hobby is its scope for creativeness and imagination. Only basic skills are called for to enhance or slightly alter a ready-to-run model loco to make it quite distinctive to an individual layout.

There are very many models available and it is not possible to cover more than a few examples here.

One of the popular modern releases is the Airfix-GMR 1400 class 0-4-2T tank engine in OO scale, which comes in GWR or BR finish, and will have been chosen to suit a period. It is a great model as it comes and some may think that is all there is to it, but it can be given an individual touch. Do not take the model for granted. Get hold of some books which show pictures of the real thing – give technical details, drawings, and many photographs. Study the pictures with the model and all sorts of things will come to light.

For a start the top feed fitting on the boiler was a

Improving the breed – 2. Close up view of a Hornby 'Schools' with missing chassis detail added, including sand box, sand pipes, front brake blocks, and brake rigging – all as yet unpainted

late addition, and many locos in the class never had it at any time. Before 1946 the number series was 48XX and not 14XX. There were no steps on the bunker sides, and at all times there was great variety in the actual placing of the tool boxes alongside the front splashers. Some locos had the auto gearbox on the front buffer beam, not the rear as in the model. And there was a whole class numbered in the 58XX series with no auto gear fitted. The GWR version of the model is suitable for the 1946–47 period only, and before that even the lettering styles differed – usually a GWR circular monogram from 1934–46 and the words 'Great Western' before that. Then all locos had a raised brass number plate, not the flat transfer applied to the model. From all this it can be seen that there is immense potential for individuality. At the simplest level, a cheap pair of etched brass number plates from the Kings Cross range can be glued over the transfers – the model looks better already! Beyond that, if a layout is set in the 1930s period, more can be done, such as removal of the GWR lettering and replacement with a GWR totem transfer, select 48XX number plates, and removal of the top feed and bunker steps, filing the sawn areas smooth and repainting the areas. Watch those toolboxes on 14XX locos. They may be further forward (or even missing) on certain locos, and so may need to be sawn off and re-sited.

So much for the prototype detail, but what about other improvements? There is little actually missing on this 1400 class 0-4-2T model. But the steam heat pipes are not supplied so one should be added at each end below the buffer beam. Then the various bunker and tank side hand rails are simply moulded into the plastic, and the model will look much better with real wire hand rails. So carve off and rub down the moulded rails, drill some locating holes, and make actual rails from wire – although for OO scale models like this one, office staples of the Rexel or Bambi variety are often just right. Next crunch up a piece of coal (with a hammer – outdoors), put the small pieces in a polythene bag for safe keeping. Smear glue over the plastic coal and sprinkle the crushed coal over this to give the bunker a realistic load. Add a driver and fireman and the model really starts to look like a working loco, not just a catalogue illustration.

Now it could be made to look a little 'used', for real locomotives, be they steam, diesel, or electric, get weathered and dirty with use even if they are cleaned quite frequently. Start off by painting the bright wheel rims and the centre hubs 'dirty black', then paint the side rods a mix of brownish black. This effects another immediate improvement in looks for it actually makes the wheels look 'finer' in scale. There is staining and discolouration from exhaust and muck thrown up from the track, quite apart from runs caused by steam or water on steam locos, grease dribbles, and much else, on even freshly painted locomotives. So long as it is not overdone, a little light work to simulate some of these effects can add greatly to the realism of a model. Skilled work with an air brush can do wonders here, but a reasonable job can be done with ordinary brushes using the 'dry brush' technique – dip only the tip of the brush in the paint, work out most of the paint on a piece of scrap, then apply the 'dirt' by very light strokes in the required area.

The technique can be practised on old discarded models or on plastic scrap. On the real thing 'wear and weathering' dirt is hard to define in terms of colour – one tends to notice the contrast colours, so on a black engine the greyish-brown staining stands out most, while on a light coloured engine the blackish-brown colours show up most. The recommended approach is to get a selection of dull matt

Improving the breed – 3. This Fleischmann Class 94 German tank locomotive has been considerably altered to a variation of the class, with new cab and bunker made from card and a grimy finish to depict a hard-worked loco

Opposite, top: classic French Nord 4–4–0 is a hand-made HO model to special order for the collector's market and reproducing all the elegance of the original

Opposite, bottom: Bavarian 2–8–0 is an example of a limited run brass model in HO made by the Swiss firm of Fulgurex

Top: a famous French type was the 141TC 2–8–2 of SNCF which worked the Paris commuter trains in the days of steam. This HE model by Ks comes as a kit of parts for home assembly

Above: one of the last steam types built, and still in service in the early 1980s, was this Class 01 4–6–2 of the East German Deutsche Reichsbahn. Model is made by Piko, in HO

Centre: the famous 'Liberation Mikado' was made in USA for delivery to French Railways in the early post-Second World War years as part of the Marshall Aid scheme. These were the last French locomotives in steam and some are still stored for possible future use. This is the fine Jouef HO model

colours – white, grey, 'track colour', black, brown, 'underframe dirt', and a useful shade from several paint makers, 'mushroom'. Make a 'palette' from a piece of card, put a blob of each colour, and use a

First large scale production diesel type for West Germany in the 1950s was the Class 221. Fleischmann model in HO scale is shown in the latest Deutsche Bundesbahn livery

brush to mix various combinations of shade as required. There may be whitish dribbles from wash-out plugs and cylinder relief valves, brownish dirt round handrails and along ledges, sooty dirt on foot-plates and tender tops, and so on. Note that fresh steam often makes the tops of boilers and cab roofs shiny in combination with an oily deposit and runs of water from tank fillers and oil from fuel fillers also shines. A neat way of simulating these is to use gloss clear varnish applied with a brush, although just a touch of Five Minute Epoxy applied with the little finger can also do the job realistically.

One point is often overlooked; check how the original was painted as compared to the model. Models often have shiny bare metal hand rails or shiny safety valves, yet the full-size loco probably has these painted to match the body colour. Just touching in these fittings can make a lot of difference. Buffer beams are another area where the style of painting on the model sometimes differs from the real thing. This is particularly so in the case of diesel locos, where there is great variety of style. On diesels and electrics, too, much attention focuses on the buffer beam, for modern locos have a mass of brake, heating, and MU control pipes, and

on most models these are missing. Likewise screen wipers and other subtle detail fittings are often omitted from models. Adding all these can quite transform the appearance of an otherwise good but unexceptionally detailed ready-to-run model.

Most of the popular French and German loco types have enormous scope for detail changes and weathering. That bright red of the chassis and running gear of German steam locos, well-known from models, is much less noticeable in real life for a patina of grime toned it down a lot and sometimes the red was not apparent at all. There were many variations in 'plumbing' on European steam locos, and any given model is usually just representative of the type. If Fleischmann's fine DB Class 94 (in HO or N scales) is taken as an example, the real thing could have had its feed-water heater (and associated piping) in any of three positions (or none at all), there were at least three combinations of bunker and cab styles, at least two styles of marking (according to period), one or two domes on the boiler, and many tiny variations. Fleischmann's model can be made to look quite distinctive by finding pictures of real locos, selecting an actual machine, and making a model look like it. This can be repeated for virtually every loco, although some like Roco's Class 23 or Liliput's Class 42, being very recent models, are so highly detailed (and include a few alternative detail parts with the model) that they need little more than weathering and the addition of coal in the tender.

Some models are produced with errors of omission or dimensions, and these may need more work. For example, many British outline models lack front steps because these would either be difficult to mould or would hinder bogie swing on tight curves. They can be made from plastic card, or taken from kits in some cases (such as the Airfix unmotorised OO loco kits), or bought as spare castings from specialist suppliers. Similarly, cylinders may be too short, glazing omitted from cabs, or brake shoes and sand boxes left off altogether. A favourite omission is sand pipes – the sand box is there but not the pipe to the wheel rim. Microrod or wire can remedy the omission but it is important with sand boxes or brake shoes to ensure that none of these additions catch on the running gear or jam the wheels. If in doubt leave this area alone.

Another problem, mainly found in British models, is an unsightly and unrealistic gap of daylight between front footplate and bogie, again to allow for bogie swing on tight curves. This can be overcome visually by cementing black plastic card strips, cut to clear the wheels, under the front footplate in line with the main frames. A few models have other errors such as a footplate which is too long, a tender which is too long, or even a footplate which is too narrow. These need more work – some addition of plastic card, and a little cutting and amending.

With ready-to-run models so widely available it is easy to forget that there are yet other types. Top of the list in terms of price and detail finish are the brass hand-made locomotives, most of which come from Japan or Korea. British and German prototypes are produced in limited numbers, but the bulk of output is American prototype in HO, O, or S. Some models are supplied painted but most are of bare or lacquered brass. Prices are high, but the quality of finish is exquisite. They are all full working models, and although most are mechanically excellent there are occasional examples where the performance is mediocre or indifferent (if purchasing, a trial run in the shop is recommended – indeed a trial with even an ordinary ready-to-run model should be possible).

A fair number of brass models are collected rather than operated and, indeed, collecting locomotives, mostly brass or other hand-crafted, hand-painted examples, is a legitimate branch of the overall model railway hobby. There are those who collect limited-production brass models and keep them as an investment, possibly buying and selling over a long period, for the values of limited production hand-made brass models rise with their scarcity. The same can be said of models made to order by specialist builders, such as Beeson, in Great Britain.

Another area where the collecting hobby has

The General Motors EMD F units were the dominant type which saw in the diesel revolution in USA and finally ousted steam. Many F unit models are available, and this F7 is by Athearn in HO scale

Collecting locomotives can become almost a hobby in its own right. Here is part of a thousand-plus collection by one modeller!

Adding passengers to miniature trains gives them a very life-like atmosphere, as shown in the Swiss TEE express made in HO scale by HAG

grown greatly in recent years is the 'tinplate' toy. The old pre-war Hornby Gauge O models, lithographed in tinplate, and delightfully made, are now sought after, as are other tinplate models of the era such as those by Bassett-Lowke, Märklin, and Lionel. Prices have soared accordingly. Yet others now collect old model locomotives of the more recent past: Hornby-Dublo, Triang, Trix Twin, and so on – all models no longer in production.

Lastly, there are kit-built model locomotives. Before the increase in the availability of ready-to-run model locos in the last ten years, one way to get variety was to buy the cast metal kits which were produced in the most popular scales. The simplest of these are 'body line' kits, containing only the superstructure. When assembled the superstructure fits over a standard ready-to-run chassis. The Hornby 0-6-0 chassis has long been a favourite for this; Wills, K's and Gem are the makers offering the biggest selection of these in OO or N (mainly Gem) for British prototype. Many other complete OO loco kits are produced, containing chassis, wheels, and sometimes motors as well as the superstructure. In some cases materials other than cast metal are used for bodies, but cast soft metal is most frequently used because its moulding and casting process lends itself most easily to short runs for a realtively small market. CCW, All-Nation, Chuffs and a few others offer similar kits for O Gauge and Gem produces some for TT. Most, however, are for HO or OO, depending on the prototype. American, French and German prototype kits exist (mostly in Britain), but nearly all cast kits are of British prototype.

Making these complete kits calls for a fair amount

of skill, though the body line kits are a much easier proposition than those for which a full chassis must be made. Cleaning up and fitting is needed with cast metal kits and as they now tend to cost more than equivalent size ready-to-run models it is worth taking time and patience over assembly.

Needless to say there are still a good many modellers who like to try scratch-building – if there is no kit or no ready-to-run example available then scratch-building will be the only way in any case. A scale drawing is the starting point, of course. Any suitable material can be used, card, plastic card, brass, or nickel-silver, to suit individual skills. Scratch-built brass chassis, wheels and motors can be obtained from specialist suppliers, and tools are required. There are a few plastic static unmotorised kits for locomotives and these have long been popular challenges for motorising or fitting to existing power chassis.

Finally, whether detailing or converting ready-to-run models, making locomotives from cast kits, or scratch-building, do remember that there is a good selection of components and detail parts available, ranging from wheels of specific types to varied chimneys, splashers, smokebox doors, brake rigging, and just about everything else to do with a locomotive exterior – even running lights and sets of fire irons. For the loco conversion enthusiast it is worth getting the catalogues of Crownline (British), Kemtron (USA), and M & F (UK/Germany) for these specialist firms produce many detail and conversion parts for specific locomotive types. Remember the loco crews too – all too many modellers forget to add men in the cab.

Rolling stock

The selection of rolling stock for a particular layout will be self-evident and catalogues show model passenger coaches (or cars) in abundance, while freight stock is even more plentiful. The only real point to emphasise is that models released in recent years are much superior to older models still on the market.

Not so long ago the British prototype modeller had a poor choice of passenger stock. Most was early BR standard stock, even if some of it was painted up to depict pre-nationalisation companies, but now all the main makers offer quite exquisite models which while they will not quite cover every requirement will satisfy almost everyone in some way. Personal research before purchasing is worthwhile, checking catalogue models against prototype information in the rolling stock books which have been published over the years. For example, if small four-wheel coaches are needed for a light railway layout, those offered by Hornby may be attractive, but these are bogus (or 'freelance') as a type, being produced in a general style to suit an existing chassis, so if the preference is something rather more authentic in the way of British four-wheelers one should look to the kits of GWR types offered by Ratio. Bogus colour schemes are widely applied to American equipment. For example, fine models of standard Pennsylvania Railroad P70 stock are produced in PRR livery, but these are also sold in the colour schemes of other big railroads which *did not* actually use them. This application of bogus colours is quite common as a commercial ploy, of course. It *is* sometimes possible to turn bogus schemes to advantage. If vans are marked for a brewery and research shows that no such vans or brewery existed in real life, the problem can be overcome by creating a brewery on a layout with an appropriate name to match the vans!

Most passenger stock is to scale length, although models of modern French or German coaches are commonly produced to a compressed 1:100 scale length instead of the correct 1:87 scale for HO, as are some for other European countries. This is because of the extreme length of the originals, which would make them look ugly on tight radius curves if modelled in the correct length. This sounds worse than it really is: all long coaches are to 1:100 scale (except for a few specialist makes) and therefore everything acquired from the major makers will be similarly reduced, providing a visual uniformity. The same ploy is used for most long modern HO passenger cars on the American market, although as there are also plenty of short prototypes to choose from on American railways there are smaller scale length cars available.

Length is a bugbear for modellers with small

Below: superb scratch-building by Gordon Heywood produced this exquisitely detailed LNWR cattle van for O Gauge

Bottom: fine detail on this Swiss baggage car by the Swiss firm of HAG includes the luggage and cycles visible when the loading doors are opened, all in 1:87 scale

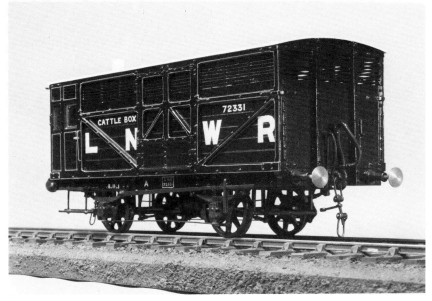

layouts, passenger stock in particular. Even a three-coach train, tiny in real life, is monstrously long on a layout only 6ft (1·83m) long! Perhaps on such a layout a single diesel railcar would be a better buy? Anything which saves length is worth going for on small compact layouts, to help the visual illusion.

Freight stock is particularly subject to the use of bogus markings, and in ready-to-run form it also suffers from production standardisation. Thus a company may offer several colourful private owner

Assembling a British Private Owner coal wagon from a Cambrian kit

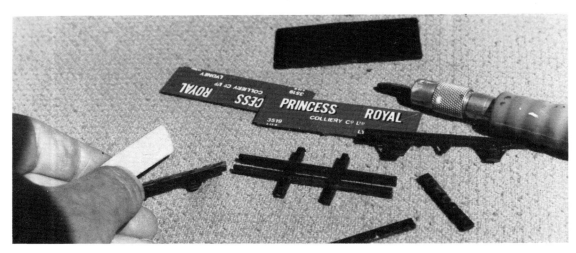

Typical American kit by Roundhouse – an HO coal hopper with pre-painted parts

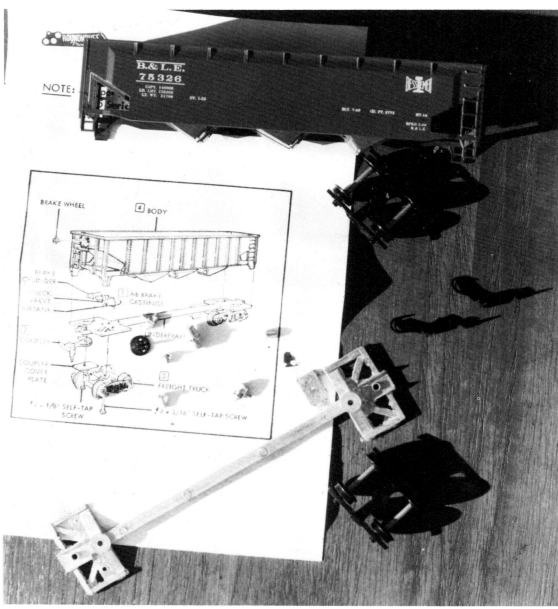

Improving ready-to-run
models with mould lines
being filed away and brake
pipes and other details added

coal wagons which look very pretty, but are all basically the same wagon on a standard chassis – the
colours and markings are the only difference. Often
the wheelbase is wrong, too. In real life these
wagons were made by several companies, all had
their own characteristics, and the detail differences
were many. Oil tank wagons are even worse offen-
ders, for any maker having tooled up to make a
particular tanker will ring the changes by issuing it
in different colours and with markings which are not
necessarily accurate for the particular colour scheme
depicted.

However, ready-to-run rolling stock does offer
excellent value for money, and most important it
usually rolls well. Ready-to-run models can be improved by cleaning up the buffer beam areas, where
there are often mould lines which should be filed off.
Roofs sometimes have a rough parting cut from the

mould which can be rubbed down. The lining of
coaches is often carried across grab handles or handrails, and hinges. Touch out the lining at such
places, for in real life it would pass underneath these
fittings. Adding a few passengers to coaches, and
luggage in guards vans (where the interior can be
seen) is a trick which really brings a train to life.
Firms like Kemco and PC produce decals which
allow end markings or set numbers to be added to
coaches and 'no smoking' or 'first' signs which can
be added to windows. Add brake and end pipes to
the buffer beam (coupling swing permitting). Paint
any bright wheels black – it immediately improves
the appearance – and do some weathering, particularly on the bogies and underframe.

Freight stock can be given similar treatment.
Smooth down mould lines on buffers and buffer
beams, blacken the wheels, and add brake pipes if

appropriate. Add guards in brake vans or conductors or conductors and brakemen/flagmen in caboose cars. Do some weathering and dirtying on all freight stock (in service virtually all freight vehicles get dirty). Floquil produce a special Polly S weathering kit, providing acrylic paints ready mixed for oil, dirty black, dust, mud and grime, while the same firm produces an aerosol 'Instant Weathering' spray (Humbrol aerosol Dark Earth is a substitute). Any acrylic or enamel paint can be used for weathering, selecting brown, black, white, etc. When a number of vehicles have been treated with brush painting, take them outdoors and give them a quick random squirt of Instant Weathering or Dark Earth. Some vehicles should be grimier than others; some can be almost ex-works, maybe with only light weathering on the chassis.

Some cheaper American and German freight vehicles are sold with catwalks and ladders added in black plastic, whereas in real life these were usually painted body colour. Modern freight vehicles sometimes run as unit trains with all stock permanently coupled. With something like a modern BR Merry-go-Round coal train or an American Great Lakes area ore train, try running vehicles permanetly coupled in at least fours for extra realism. Discard the auto-couplers and use wire loop-and-hook (home made) or Roco short couplers to replace them. Only the auto-couplers on the other vehicles of each rake need to be retained. This can also be done on fixed rakes of passenger stock. Finally, provide loads for all open vehicles as appropriate. Most makers actually provide removable loads for some vehicles, and accessory firms make dummy loads to fit the most common models. But such loads are easy enough to make at home using balsa wood cut to size, with legs to hold it at the correct height. Paint the wood to match the load (eg, black for coal) then glue crushed material (eg, coal, gravel, ballast, etc) on top of it. Loads of barrels and crates are also sold separately, but they can be made up in a similar fashion by glueing them to a card base. Timber or log loads are simply cut from balsa strip or twigs and glued or bound in clusters.

Most modellers add kit-built rolling stock to their collections. Such models tend to have a lot more individuality, partly because they are less familiar and partly because building them demands a certain amount of skill. Kits are hardly found in Continental Europe (probably because so many ready-to-run vehicles are available). For British and American prototypes, however, kits abound. Athearn, Roundhouse, Trains-Miniature, Walthers and Silver Streak are the big names in the USA (although there are many others), and Peco, Cambrian, Ratio, 3H, Slaters and Wrightlines are among many British producers. Standards are high and the leading names are not likely to disappoint. Most are extremely easy to make, especially the American ones, and nearly all American and several British kits also come fully coloured. Kit vehicles are generally more authentic than the ready-to-run vehicles because they are modelled on specific types and are seldom designed to utilise common chassis and fittings.

Coach kits are sometimes rather more difficult

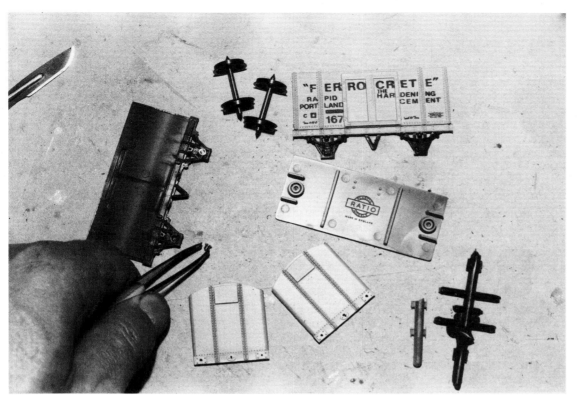

Opposite, top: simple dirt application. Paint on matt black and quickly wipe it off again with a tissue or cloth. Note bright wheels are painted black. Do not forget the insides of freight vehicles, such as coal hoppers

Opposite, centre: use 'dry brushing' technique to apply streaky runs and spillage to hoppers and freight vehicles of all kinds

Opposite, bottom: finish off with a quick squirt of 'instant weathering' or dark earth from an aerosol spray applied from below to simulate dirt thrown up from the track – this could be applied by brush instead

Left: assembling a Ratio Iron Mink kit, showing scrap weights added to improve its running qualities

than freight stock kits, often because they require more finishing off. In the case of British OO, the Ratio model coaches are plastic construction kits of short prototypes, and are worth a look by anyone considering coaching stock.

As with everything else in this hobby one can work from scratch as well. Everything needed in the way of wheels, bogies, trucks, couplings, axle-boxes, strapping, brake gear, and many other items can be obtained from the larger model railway specialist shops. The model magazines publish scale draw-ings, and there are books and specialist suppliers where further scale drawings can be obtained. Card, plastic card, or wood can be used, or a combination of all three. A few old litho or pre-printed card sets are still to be had where the sides and ends of wagons are supplied in full colour for addition as overlays to scratch-built bodies. Some enthusiasts scratch-build highly detailed vehicles as a major part of their involvement in the hobby – others are content to use or modify the ready-to-run offerings. The choice, again, is for the individual.

Couplers and signals

Couplers are a problem for all model railway fans some time or other, although the situation is not too bad if the limitations of miniaturising a railway system are accepted. The reason why model railway couplers do not resemble those of the full-size trains is to be found in the track radius (curvature). In Europe most trains couple with a chain and hook, and normally these days the coupler is tightened with a screw-link, although loose coupling is still occasionally seen. Buffers on adjacent wagons may just about touch, and they will certainly bang together as the train moves off, for they are spring loaded as well.

Real railways have a minimum allowed radius for curved track, and this scales down to 10ft (3·05m) radius in OO scale. Thus a simple circle of track would need to be 20ft (6·10m) across. And these figures are for the absolute minimum radius. Few people could find room for a layout big enough to reproduce curves to scale radius (or scale length come to that – around 80ft (24m) for a single scale mile). So model railway tracks have a much smaller radius, which looks reasonably effective and allows layouts to fit into reasonable areas. In practice OO/HO model track is sold from 10in (254mm) radius up to about 2ft (0·6m) radius for sectional track. Curves laid with flextrack to 3–4ft (0·9–1·2m) radius are considered generous and tend to be found only on larger layouts. Faced with curves sharper than this, vehicles fitted with scale couplers suffer from buffer-locking and swift derailment, as the buffer faces slide off each other on a curve and jam together instead.

The auto-coupler was introduced quite early on in the model rail hobby to prevent buffer-locking. In effect the auto-coupler holds adjacent vehicles apart far enough to prevent the buffers touching. The British market saw the introduction of the tension-lock coupler by Hornby (then Triang) around 1958 and this has become virtually the standard for all British models in TT3 and OO scales. There have been several refinements, such as the introduction of slightly smaller versions, plus a 'quick' release' slot recently introduced by Hornby to assist hand uncoupling. With few exceptions today, every British outline OO/HO model has this type of coupler and all makes are compatible although some are less attractive than others.

Advantages for the tension-lock coupler are the 'hands off' operation and the ease with which uncoupling ramps can be positioned and used with no need of further wiring. Uncoupling ramps are spring loaded and should need no further attention once positioned in track. The ramp only works when the coupler is held on the ramp, so there is no danger of spontaneous uncoupling. The absence of an uncoupler ramp can be taken care of by hand uncoupling. A screwdriver or a 'portable' ramp consisting of an old ball pen with a plastic card 'plate' glued to the bottom, can be used to assist uncoupling in the absence of nearby ramps.

The other well-known type of British coupler is the Simplex, made by Peco but used years ago by Trix, Hornby-Dublo, and others. This coupler is very good and much less conspicuous than the tension-lock. It needs a sideways operating action and is designed with a knuckle so that adjacent vehicles are not disturbed when any vehicle is lifted right out of the train. An uncoupling ramp is available for the Simplex, too, from Peco. However, no ready-to-run models now come in OO size with a Simplex type coupler so that if the Simplex is used all vehicles have to be refitted, since it is not compatible with the tension-lock coupler.

The alternative to the Simplex is the Magni-Simplex, also made by Peco. This is a claw-type coupler with a metal vertical operating bar. When

Right: the neat Peco Magni-Simplex coupler, shown with the magnet which operates it

Opposite: on John Pomeroy's OO Gauge layout where curves are gentle, scale 3-link couplers are used. Even so a wire bar is soldered between the buffers to prevent buffer-locking

two wagons are stopped over a magnet, set into the track, the old physics law of 'like poles repel' comes into effect. The two vertical bars swing apart and release the coupler claws. For fly shunting an uncoupled wagon can be pushed along by the loco and released by stopping the loco so that the wagon runs on into the appropriate siding. Obviously a special magnet is needed in the track at each uncoupling point. The coupler fits easily to Peco's own range of model wagons but it is not always easy to fit to other makes due to the widely differing ways of mounting the tension-lock couplers.

There are several other makes of OO (4mm scale) coupler of which the Sprat and Winkle type is the best known and most widely used. It is not always easy to fit, but it has the advantage of being much less conspicuous than any other auto-coupler type. The prominent over-scale size of auto-couplers in general is what makes most people who worry about it seek something better. The ultimate alternative for OO is the scale 3-link coupler which fits into a slot in the buffer beam and is sprung just like the real thing. The original type of 3-link coupler is somewhat over-scale itself, and many now prefer the Protofour type which is an exact scale replica. Screw-type couplers, mostly dummy, are also available for locos and passenger stock fitted with this type of coupler.

A problem with scale couplers is the buffer-locking which happens when trains are backed, and may well happen even when trains are pulled. A minimum radius of 3ft is needed to avoid constant trouble in OO. However, soldering a wire or glueing a strip of Microrod across the face of the buffers will help solve the buffer-locking problem without really detracting from appearance. The wire or bar will

stop the buffers slipping inside each other. With this bar in place it is possible to use 3-link couplers even on track with a radius of 2ft or less, although as the buffers are unsprung there may then be the problem of derailments because there is no 'give' in the system. Given the work and problems involved it is easy to see why so many modellers are content with auto-couplers even if they are over-scale.

To all this can be added the fiddling problem of hooking up scale couplings in OO size. A wire hook is needed and there is a version available attached to a penlight which throws a beam on to the coupler. Also the Protofour coupler is magnetised so that it stays with the coupling hook and does not drop half way through the coupling operation.

For HO in Continental Europe there are two widely used auto-couplers. Most common is the NEM Class A type, used by all but one maker. This is essentially a hook with a lifting loop: push two vehicles together and the loop lifts to drop over the adjacent hook. Narrow gauge HOe and HOm models have a similar type of coupler, much reduced in size. This coupler has a metal loop and plastic hook. In some forms (eg, Rivarossi) it will uncouple magnetically by stopping the wagons over a magnet so that the two loops lift. Alternatively an uncoupling ramp can be used. Available from several makers in manual or remote electric forms, this ramp must be raised to operate, making this type of coupler less convenient to use than the British tension-lock. Using a small screwdriver one can uncouple manually by lifting both loops.

The alternative to the NEM Class A type coupler is the Fleischmann type. This is a hook-and-bar coupler rather like a much smaller version of the British tension lock. Being less conspicuous it is

Horn-hook couplers are fitted on this super-detailed B & O C–16 'Little Joe'

probably the best of all the mechanical auto-couplers and it is certainly the neatest. It also needs a raised ramp (manual or electric) to work it since the tail of the hook is not long enough to reach a sprung ramp as in the British tension-lock system. Almost all makers in Europe design their models to be fitted with either coupler and firms like Roco and Piko supply some of their models with both. Hence one can standardise on the preferred system.

A third alternative is the Roco 'close coupler', a very inconspicuous slotted type of coupler which is also spring-mounted so that on sharp curves the gap between vehicles opens out to suit, then closes down to scale distance a notably superior method. Roco produce versions to fit all their vehicles, and many others as well.

In the United States the coupler systems are different again, but very much easier. The common type used by all ready-to-run suppliers is called the horn-hook, a fair replica of a knuckle type auto-coupler except that it has a long side 'horn' to catch the adjacent coupler and a vertical tail to work on the uncoupling ramp. This horn-hook is cheap and effective when vehicles are run together. So long as the spring does not break or the mounting drop out of line it is not likely to get trouble. On many freight and passenger cars the coupler is mounted above the truck (bogie) rather than on the chassis frame, so that very sharp curves can be negotiated without trouble. Simple plastic uncoupler ramps are available cheaply to fit inside the tracks. However, uncoupling is the least satisfactory feature of a horn-

hook; it has a sideways spring action and in going over an uncoupling ramp a complete vehicle might be forced sideways off the track if the tail of the coupler fails to engage the ramp properly, and unless the couplers are exactly in line the uncoupling action will not work either. Horn-hooks can be uncoupled satisfactorily by hand by pushing down from above with an ice lolly stick which has been split diagonally in half (push the point between the 'hooks' of the two couplers and twist, and the two couplers will be forced apart).

The major alternative to the horn-hook is the Kadee magnetic, an excellent coupler that looks just like a real knuckle coupler and operates in the same way as the Magni-Simplex (the Kadee preceded the Magni-Simplex type on the market by many years). The coupler is fitted using a gauge to ensure correct height. Magnets in the track cause the couplers to open. The vertical tail that is moved by the magnet is shaped to resemble the air brake hose which hangs there on the real thing.

Kadee also produce a version with a long shank for use with European vehicles. Bear in mind that knuckle type auto-couplers are increasingly used in real life in Europe these days (eg, on British coaches) so the use of the Kadee couplers can be entirely true to prototype.

All the foregoing applies only to HO/OO and TT Gauge models, except where noted. In N Gauge virtually all makers have standardised on a neat coupler originated by Arnold, the pioneer N Gauge makers. This is best described as a 'sprung knuckle'

Kadee coupler on a British OO wagon at the right, compared on left with early Airfix version of the tension-lock coupler which is also similar to the Fleischmann version

Magnet set in track showing
Kadee coupler displaced
sideways (to uncouple from
adjacent vehicle) due to
magnetic force

Using a cocktail stick to
uncouple the standard N
Gauge coupler by hand

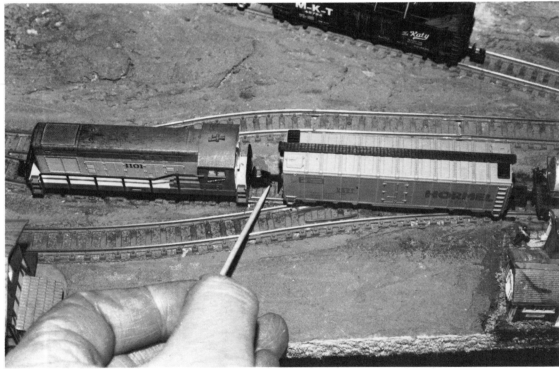

with bevelled faces which ride over each other. It is simple and effective but again depends on a manual or remote control raised ramp for uncoupling – less than satisfactory, for a badly placed ramp can end up lifting the entire vehicle off the track. Many modellers uncouple by hand and a wood cocktail stick is a good tool for lifting and separating the little couplers without touching the vehicles.

Roco have a short 'close coupler' for N Gauge similar to the HO version and this is certainly an improvement in visual terms as it is much more slender than the Arnold coupler. In the USA Kadee

make the N scale version of their fine magnetic coupler, offering it with various types of mounting but, for N scale only, already mounted on bogies (trucks) or in adaptor kits for fitting to various N Gauge American locomotives.

In Gauge 1, Märklin offer a coupler which is similar to the Arnold N Gauge type, very neat and with a handle to assist in manual uncoupling. Gauge O commercial models by Lima and others have a Simplex-type coupler similar to the HO/OO Peco version but much bigger. Some American O Gauge models have the Lionel style of coupler which just about joins with the Simplex type. Most Gauge O and Gauge 1 modellers use scale 3-link couplers, however, and in America Kadee offer a good magnetic knuckle coupler.

In Gauge Z Märklin offer a claw-type auto-coupler which is obtrusive on a single vehicle but is much less obvious on a coupled train. Märklin also list an uncoupling ramp to work this coupler.

Summing up, couplers can give trouble if one tries to mix too many makes. Market forces, however, almost determine the choice if the facility of auto-coupling is required. The British tension-lock idea is the best in terms of fool-proof working, even though it is obtrusive in appearance. Almost all couplers have many pros and cons and it is up to the individual to decide the choice.

Tight radius curves (less than 3ft radius) require the use of auto-couplers since 3-link couplers would not work satisfactorily. It is worth mentioning that certain couplers, such as the tension-lock or NEM Class A do not need both hooks or loops to work. Therefore it is possible, at least on loco front ends, to remove the hook or loop as necessary so that front end appearance is to some extent improved. Obviously the hook or loop must be left on the adjacent vehicle to engage the loco. Some loco-motive models are actually sold with a simplified front coupler while some are sold with no front coupler at all.

Signals In theory, it is easy enough to add the right signals to suit a given layout, but it is rare for any modeller to get to the stage of authentic signalling. There is so much else to do that signals have low priority, while most lay-outs, even quite big ones, are so compressed in the actual run of trackage that putting in all the correct signals would crowd them ridiculously.

With a branch line, short line, or light railway layout it may be possible to get away with no signals at all, except perhaps where the main line is reached (here a signal might guard the junction). But lines like this might have no other signals because they operate 'one engine in steam' and all turn-outs are also thrown by hand or from a 'ground frame' rather than a signal box. Other lines, even on main routes, might be single line where the token system is in operation from section to section, again with simpli-fied signalling. Hence, depending on the layout, it may be feasible to overlook the signals or reduce them to a minimum.

Many modellers use signals purely for cosmetic decoration. On a typical small layout, like that shown on page 74, signals are added at the station (in the 'starter' position) to give an impression of a signalling system for a 'cross-country' railway, even if the signals do not actually link with the turn-outs, or relate to any sectionalising. On the layout drawn the signals are wired for remote operation, but could equally well be static, or hand-worked.

In general signalling systems are the same the world over, although the appearance changes from country to country. In essence, signals exist for safety reasons and they guide the train driver along the route. Real railways are sectionalised into 'blocks' with only one train allowed in any section at any one time. They are also linked to locks on the turn-outs so that, for example, if a signal is 'on' (set for danger) the turn-out ahead of it is locked also.

Signals generally are of the mechanical sema-phore type or colour light type. In each section of track the simplest set up will be a 'distant' signal which warns of the likely state of the next signal. In Britain the 'distant' is a yellow arm (or yellow light) and when 'on' at danger it can be passed but it indicates that the next signal, the 'home' signal, is likely to be set at danger too. As this is a red arm (or red/green light) signal trains must stop until the

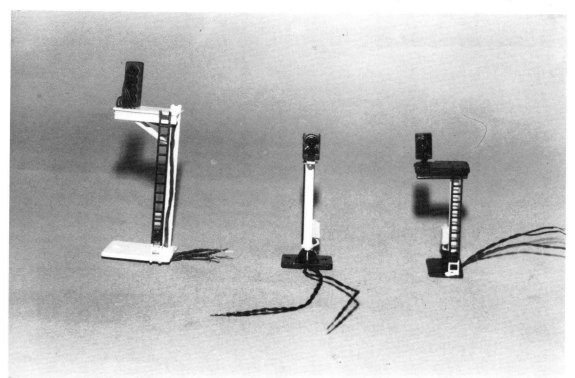

Working colour light signals from the EPC range

signal goes 'off' (green light showing) allowing the train to proceed. Next, beyond the station will be a 'starter' signal with the same conditions, after which the train may pass into the next section. Branch lines, junctions, or sidings are all protected by signals with similar rules, and ground or disc signals cover secondary shunting movements.

Quite a long run of track would be necessary to fit in the full sequence of signals at credible spacings. Hence if a layout depicts only a section of track near a station one might choose to model only the 'starter' signal at the station and possibly the 'distant' signal as the track exits from view at a tunnel mouth. Junctions and branches can also be signalled. Few modellers with small layouts would link these (interlock them) with related turn-outs as there is extra electrical complication. Fleischmann, Märklin and others who offer the parts for a miniature block system make provision for interlocking signals and turn-outs with all the necessary plug-in components.

British terms have so far been used to describe signals, but other countries use similar systems with different names. For example, in Germany, a 'hauptsignal' is roughly equivalent to a 'home' signal, and in USA various names are used, such as 'stop and proceed' for what the British call 'distant', 'approach' for what the British call 'home' and 'clear' for 'starter'.

The system covered so far is the block system, but a modern development of this, possible in the age of computers and electronics, is centralised traffic control (CTC – also known by other terms) where the number of signal boxes on a route are greatly reduced or eliminated. A controller with a computerised display panel hundreds of miles away can control trains over the whole route, and this may lead to a reduction in the number of sections on the route as a whole and therefore in the number of signals. This is another let-out for the modeller of the modern scene, for signal boxes may be omitted and a few cosmetic colour light signals can be positioned on the pretext that the layout is just part of an overall CTC system.

Another signal system of interest, and easy for modellers to simulate, is the old American train order system. In its simplest form each station had a dispatcher in telegraphic link with the next section down the line. With huge single track mileages to cover, trains ran in each direction from passing siding to passing siding. A dispatcher receiving a train on one direction knew where the next train was as it approached from the opposite direction. He could adjust progress by passing a 'train order' to the driver – such as 'Wait at Cook's Siding for southbound train No. 10 to pass'. If one train was running late the actual passing place could be adjusted so that the other train was not held up. Hence the familiar train order signal at typical American stations with the signal arm held vertical to indicate that a new train order is to be picked up. Orders might indicate extra stopping places also or late changes of pick-up for freight. Out in the country there might be only the train order system in operation, but generally it was combined with block signalling. Most American signalling today, however, is on CTC lines.

Signals themselves are widely available in model form. Of particular note are excellent kits by Ratio for working OO semaphore signals, but both light and semaphore signals are produced in nearly every ready-to-run range. Some are rather cruder than others, particularly those which are remotely operated, for they may have heavy bases to take power leads and these may need disguising for extra realism. On the other hand modern electronic miniaturisation makes possible some superior ranges of electric colour light signals which are to fine scale even though they carry electric circuits. Some of these, such as Märklin's Gauge 1 German versions, are exquisite models, fully wired for remote working and in every way accurate.

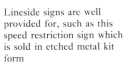

Lineside signs are well provided for, such as this speed restriction sign which is sold in etched metal kit form

Operating a layout

It has been emphasised throughout this book that the many aspects of railway modelling are closely related, and to get the best from the hobby it is important to integrate them. There is no point in rushing out to buy a complete ten coach express train set in OO Gauge, for example, if the only space available for a layout is a 4ft (1·22m) long window ledge; it is wiser to find a type of railway operation which would fit into the space, and buy equipment accordingly.

A particular case in point is the relationship of a chosen track plan to the type of operation it allows – there is a tendency, even among experienced practical modellers, to overlook this, because all too many books of track plans and layout plans in magazines simply give track formations which fit certain areas with no related text to outline operating potential (or limitations). The impression is often given that the designer merely filled the space with track, and beginners can find a track plan (often quite complex) which suits their area, then copy the layout without much further thought.

This is *not* the best approach: it is far better to analyse the operating potential of every layout and choose one which allows one to do more than run trains round in circles when the layout is finished. Very often, the end result could be quite a simple track plan, probably simpler than some of those in layout books, but there will be satisfaction of knowing that everything serves a purpose, and probably reproduces real railway practice quite closely.

The key is to reproduce what real railways do – shift revenue-earning traffic. On even the simplest branch line, therefore, look for industries and facilities which will require constant traffic. Quite a few charming branch lines were actually too quiet and sleepy to offer much real life operation – that is why a lot of them closed down! One real British branch line which survived into the 1970s was the Culm Valley Branch, and it existed so long because it served an important dairy. But even that branch was restricted in operation in its latter years after passenger and general freight carriage was withdrawn.

However, it can provide inspiration for a layout based on the Culm Valley over the years, and drawing 13.1 shows a plan for a model of the terminus at Hemyock with all features of the branch at the height of its commercial success (there is even a chance (in siding 7) to add an extra facility which never existed).

The Hemyock plan shows first that there was a passenger service from the station which was operated by a single short brake/3rd coach (four-wheelers in the old days). A parcels office was also located in the station. The big dairy was the main source of freight traffic, with at least two trains a day of milk tankers or Siphons. There was a seed and feed merchant who in real life rarely had rail shipments, the cattle dock is self-explanatory, while the engine shed required occasional loads of 'loco coal' for its coaling stage. The general siding 7 was used for everything else. Coal merchant's bins or even a small grain elevator could be added although neither existed in real life. This identifies at least seven sources of traffic – milk, 'feed and seed and fertilisers', parcels, passengers, coal and general merchandise, and cattle. Of these the milk is the most important freight item. With only five turn-outs in station limits this layout is as simple as it can be for such a busy place. The run-around loop is very short – only one coach long – but it was short in real life, as was the station platform. Mixed trains were a feature of the working – freight vehicles tacked on behind the coach – and the train worked other stations up the line. The plan shows two of the little halts, each with a goods siding (coal and general merchandise), as other destinations for traffic.

This layout can get very congested indeed and will keep an operator very busy with only one engine and 6–12 wagons of suitable type. There are books which cover the Culm Valley Branch and one, *Great Western Branch Termini Vol. 2* (OPC) even includes

Drawing 13.1: layout based on the Hemyock terminus of the Culm Valley Branch

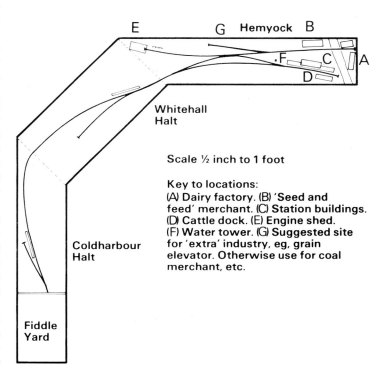

E   G   Hemyock   B

Whitehall
Halt

Scale ½ inch to 1 foot

Key to locations:
(A) Dairy factory. (B) 'Seed and feed' merchant. (C) Station buildings. (D) Cattle dock. (E) Engine shed. (F) Water tower. (G) Suggested site for 'extra' industry, eg, grain elevator. Otherwise use for coal merchant, etc.

Coldharbour
Halt

Fiddle
Yard

a timetable which could be followed exactly when operating, although there is a lot of fun inventing a timetable (or more specifically an operating sequence), then working it.

The way to approach this is to list all the facilities, then decide how busy they are going to be. Thus at Hemyock the dairy requires two trains a day – say a morning train collecting churns of milk (Siphon traffic) and an evening train collecting loaded milk tankers. As drawn the capacity of the siding is one Siphon or two tankers at most. Thus to provide for the traffic four milk tankers and two Siphons are needed (to allow exchange of loaded and empty vehicles though you can get away with half that). The morning train brings in two empty tankers and exchanges them for the loaded Siphon from the siding where it has been left overnight. The Siphon works back to Tiverton Junction (the fiddle yard on this layout). The evening milk run collects the two tankers which have been filled up during the day and leaves a Siphon overnight for the morning churn traffic, so the cycle is repeated next day.

It can be assumed that the 'seed and feed' merchant has delivery of one box van loaded with bagged fertiliser once a week, and that it takes a full 24 hours to unload. So this van comes in one day and is collected the next for return to Tiverton as an empty. Another van comes in with assorted farm items on another day each week for a 24-hour unloading. In season potatoes and other farm produce is shipped out by the same merchant, necessitating two vans daily for three weeks at a time in addition to the regular weekly vans.

There is an interesting complication here – the 'feed and seed' merchant is on the same siding as the dairy. So every time the loco has to exchange dairy traffic, twice daily, it needs to pull out any box vans standing at the 'feed and seed' merchant's loading platform. When the dairy traffic is exchanged, the 'feed and seed' van(s) must be re-positioned at the loading platform. This adds more interesting shunting.

Next assume one wagon of 'loco coal' to be required for the engine shed each week. This coal must be shovelled out on to the coaling stage in the engine shed spur, but it takes 24 hours, so the wagon must be pulled out of the siding overnight while the loco uses the shed after the last train of the day. Assume the local coal merchant takes two wagon loads of coal on Tuesdays and Fridays and these also require 24 hours to unload. Finally assume cattle transactions via the local market every Wednesday, requiring at least four cattle wagons that day.

Moving on to Whitehall Halt a coal merchant there requires one wagon load of coal a week while a farm machinery firm takes delivery of equipment there from Lowmacs. At Coldharbour the siding is used for general freight traffic. So the workings must allow for serving these sidings as well.

By the time all this has been worked out, the number of freight vehicles needed to maintain a full service will be known (one can cheat a little at first, and use a couple of box vans, say, to do the work of six, just as the layout will be built over a period of time).

The next move is to work out a practical working

'Operating' should include the art of getting all the incidental details correct to make the operations look convincing. For example, road vehicles in period with the trains, likewise posters and street furniture. On this Derby Museum layout the correct dress of passengers sets the period firmly about 1905-8

timetable or sequence. Moves for the rest of the trains through the day quickly starts to fill several sheets of paper. For example the 9.00 am train arrives at Tiverton Junction at 9.45 am (say). The loco then collects from Tiverton sidings a loaded 'loco coal' wagon, three loaded coal wagons, and a box van and brake van forming the morning freight train. This sets off down the line at 10.15 and drops off one coal wagon in the siding at Whitehall, collecting an empty in its place. Arriving at Hemyock it puts the 'loco coal' wagon into the engine shed siding and the other two coal wagons into the general siding, exchanging for, perhaps, one empty coal wagon. The box van is exchanged for one with the 'feed and seed' merchant. Time now is 11.15. The loco now runs the empties back to Tiverton, arriving at 12.00. It picks up the single coach from the passenger bay there at 12.30, changes crews perhaps, and works back to Hemyock arriving as the 1.15 pm. That completes half a 'working day' on the branch, the loco has been busy all the time and all the stock has needed to be ready.

On a layout like this a check can be kept on all the stock without paperwork. But a simple 'card order' system can duplicate the real life manifest and order system which the goods yard clerk would work out for billing purposes. It combines it with the traffic departments' records in this simple model idea. Basically, for every wagon make out a small card identifying it primarily by the number on the wagon and describing it by type and purpose.

The back of the same card can be used as a record for repairs, date of purchase, date of repaint, and so

on. For each facility on the line, eg, Dairy, Feed and Seed Merchants, make another clearly titled card. Mark on this frequency of traffic or the actual trains which serve it. Any other operator who helps on the layout thus has a cross-check on the service from this card if it is not written down elsewhere.

For a very simple layout the system is not strictly necessary, but if you expand the layout to take in further stations down the line or use the system on a larger layout with, say, six destinations, then it really comes into its own. It duplicates some of the real-life paperwork, albeit only in a simple way which keeps track of all the stock, and with such a scheme every single wagon has a purpose and an identity, and freight vehicles are no longer just decorative additions for locomotives to haul about in an aimless fashion. Everything is going somewhere just like on a real railway.

This scheme of operating can be extended to every layout which has actual identifiable starting points and destinations, and facilities for traffic exchange however complicated or simple they may be. A very precise example is shown by a layout built by the author in N Gauge – a layout of the very simplest type yet with a very busy operating schedule indeed.

The Warren, Beresford and Chicago layout was designed to provide interest in operation as well as in construction, and the operating concept of the layout was evolved to fulfil the basic aim of carrying people and goods from one point to another. This layout is the most basic form of railway, a simple single track branch line doing exactly that, carrying

Left: appropriate traffic can be allocated to the facilities on any layout. This quarry on the Michael Andress layout uses a Pola kit-built tippler with minor changes. While stone is shipped out in open wagons, explosives must be delivered for mining operations in a gunpowder van

Below: a good example of adapted kits used in an original way. This timber merchant's yard by Michael Andress uses parts from Airfix service station, coal office, and platform canopy kits, plus some balsa wood, to make typical storage sheds. The Scotch Derrick is made from balsa strip and the traction engine and pick-up truck are conversions from die-cast toys. Siding is narrow gauge but this facility is just as suitable for standard gauge

Following pages: finely detailed plastic kits from firms such as Faller, Pola, and Kibri, allow realistic German town and city scenes to be created. The station is built entirely from a kit

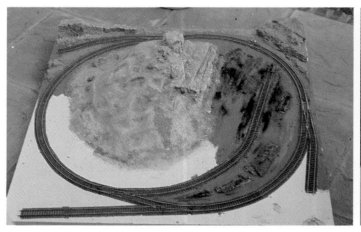

Stages in building the Willow Valley
Railway: track laid and ballasted and
basic scenery applied to the centre
and top half of the board, remainder
still bare insulation board

Level crossings added, rest of
board given scenic covering
but not surface texture, and
coal added on spoil heaps

All scenic texturing is now
complete, the buildings are in place,
trees and foliage and many details
are yet to be added, but the layout
is sufficiently finished for full
operating to get under way

The Willow Valley Light Railway is
operated by the GWR, period
1946–47, in a quiet corner of the
Forest of Dean. On a warm
afternoon it's quite a pleasant spot!

But as an alternative, the Willow
Valley Railway is a busy short line
in Virginia or Pennsylvania, time the
present or the recent past. WV
No 2, hauling coal to the main line
interchange, is an elderly Alco S2

No 5800 is a conversion from the
Airfix 1400 class 0–4–2T. It
provides half the motive power
allocated by the GWR to operate
the Willow Valley Light Railway
which serves coal mines in the
Forest of Dean, period 1946–47

Heavy limestone traffic in Derbyshire is a typical type of operation on Bill Hudson's Ashover EM Gauge layout

goods and people from an 'off-stage' location (the equivalent of the fiddle yard on the classic branch line terminus type of layout) to the stations and depots on the board. From here it is a matter of choosing a location for the line: a completely mythical line with a 'company' name of its own, or a suitable railway to which a 'branch' can be connected as a fictional addition.

This led to the idea of a 'fictional addition' to a real railway. It was necessary to find a railway which would lend itself to a simple compact branch line, offer a busy service in real life, and enable the use of ready-to-run N scale items with a minimum of adaptation. One line which fitted these requirements was the Chicago North Western Railroad which operates out of Chicago, west and north-west as its name implies. All the locomotives and stock required to operate a CNW layout are readily available in current N Gauge production, even though a

little repainting and adaptation may be necessary. Above all, the CNWR operated a commuter service into Chicago which ran further out into the country than any of the other lines in the area with commuter service.

By American standards the commuter trains offer a very frequent service and these trains operated by double-decker (or bi-level) cars are short. So a branch line similar to the Lake Geneva branch offered the idea of a modern era setting, with short trains, which could be dovetailed neatly into the existing network. The sketch map of the CNW routes (drawing 13.2), over which a commuter service operates, shows the mythical branch added to the system, running to Warren (and North Warren – freight only) from Chrystal Lake. This branch lends itself so well to existing CNW operations that it was possible to produce a passenger schedule quite readily.

To operate the layout with a logical schedule of runs a mundane working timetable is needed. As this is only the simplest of single line branches, on which it is physically impossible to run more than one train at a time, the timetable can be simple.

Time, real or speeded up, can be forgotten since this is a layout for leisurely home operation. There are nominated arrival and departure times for all the trains operating in a sequence throughout the day, but these times are descriptive rather than actual. The working timetable shows that the first train in the 24 hour weekday schedule is the 2.18 am arrival in Warren from Chrystal Lake – representing the connecting train (at Chrystal Lake) with the last train of the day out of Chicago. So an operating session can start with this train, and it is simply the 2.18 am, no matter what time the session starts.

Obviously, to work this out it was necessary to know some basic timings and to make some assumptions. So to start with train schedules for all the

commuter runs on the CNW network were acquired. Using the train schedule for the Chicago-Harvard route (on which line is the all-important Chrystal Lake junction) it is easy enough to plot the frequency of passenger trains to and from the CNW station in Chicago. An early assumption was dictated by the limited trackage at Warren; because there are no spare sidings at Warren it is not possible to have passenger trains 'laying over' waiting for their next turn, except for the last train at night which could lay over to become the first train in the morning.

The other point peculiar to the CNW operation is that all trains are made up of bi-level (double-deck) cars and are push-pull operated using F7 or E8 diesel locomotives. So there is no need for the locomotive to run around the train at Warren. On the actual CNW commuter routes there may have been anything from two to six passenger cars, the outer one a driving unit, depending on the density of the

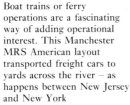

Boat trains or ferry operations are a fascinating way of adding operational interest. This Manchester MRS American layout transported freight cars to yards across the river – as happens between New Jersey and New York

Drawing 13.2: sketch map
locating the mythical Warren
Branch with actual Chicago
North Western Railway
branches NW of Chicago

route. A single car is not usual, but may be seen on late or holiday workings on some routes. For the compact Warren branch it was decided that a single trailer would be used for early and late trains running to Chrystal Lake only and two trailers would be used for trains running 'through' to Chicago. This is actually a happy assumption. As Chrystal Lake is on the Harvard-Chicago main line, with a very frequent commuter train service, it can be reasoned that trains coming off the Warren branch would not be likely to duplicate runs to Chicago. So only the most important trains run 'through' to Chicago and for the rest the passengers boarding at Warren and Beresford change at Chrystal Lake to a train already running on the Harvard-Chicago route.

Having placed all the key passenger train times at what is roughly the correct timing by real CNW standards, it was then possible to pencil in all the freight train timings on the branch. It is most unlikely there would ever be 'through' freight workings on a small branch like this. So it was assumed that all freight cars for on-line customers or facilities are dropped or picked up overnight by main line freight trains at the Chrystal Lake interchange sidings, then brought up the branch by a small locomotive assigned to the branch.

It so happens that the invented timings dove-tail quite neatly with the passenger trains, but the assumption must be made from the timings that some of the freight trains must go into passing loops or sidings down the branch to let passenger trains through. Also ignored for the present is the fact that somewhere along the 18 miles of track between Warren and Chrystal Lake there may be other on-line industries with traffic to exchange and so make further complications.

Of particular interest is the complication with the 9.45 am local freight. Long before it can finish its work at Warren and North Warren, the 10.18 am passenger train is due. So the freight locomotive has to clear the station tracks and in practice it goes round to North Warren and the train crew take a coffee break until the passenger train has departed again as the 10.35 am.

Following the American style, each train working is given a number, odd numbers out from Chicago and Chrystal Lake, even numbers inbound. The prefix '9' is supposed to indicate the line or branch – in this case the Warren branch. Actually this reference number is much easier to follow and remember than the time of the train and in practice the number is used rather than the time. Thus the 9.45 am referred to above is called Train No. 911. A

full weekday schedule has no less than 34 workings – 17 in each direction, and it takes a very full evening operating session to get through it all. Sometimes, in fact, it is not completed, but the beauty of the system is it can start and stop when and how one pleases. In CNW parlance the push-pull commuter trains are known as 'scoots' (because they scoot along quite fast!) and to save time on the timetable all passenger trains are marked as 'scoots'. The working timetable reoroduced here should be self-explanatory.

Any trains that take a personal fancy can be run on this type of layout without fundamentally changing the timetable – a modern Chicago and North Western Railroad setting is only an example. With appropriate adaptations the line could be set in France or Scotland or Germany, and the basic principles of the operation would remain the same.

Even a very simple layout like this, little more

Working timetable for the Warren Branch Layout. For track plan of this layout, see page 34

Operating the Warren Branch
Opposite, top, left: train No 909 sets off up the branch from the fiddle yard spur . . .
Opposite, top, right: . . . and at Warren, the three loaded hoppers at the mine are exchanged for the two empty hoppers from train 909
Opposite, centre, left: Scoot No 913 arrives from Chicago at 10.18 am. It will return at 10.35 am to Chicago (a push-pull working) as train 914
Opposite, centre, right: meanwhile the freight loco switches the North Warren sidings, and here exchanges tank cars at the Shell oil depot
Opposite, bottom, left: overall view of nearly all the 3ft × 2ft (0·91m × 0·61m) layout shows the Scoot occupying Warren station as it waits to push back to Chicago. Meanwhile the Fairbanks-Morse switcher loco is laying up at the North Warren sidings, pausing in its activities until the line is clear to return to Warren
Opposite, bottom, right: 'Card Orders' alongside the vehicles they refer to on the author's Warren Branch which uses the system described in the text

WORKING TIMETABLE — WARREN

No.	Time (Warren)	From	To	Duty/Remarks
901	2.18 am	C	W	Scoot — lays over at W
902	5.45 am	W	CL	Scoot — shuttle to CL and return to W
903	6.10 am	CL	W	Scoot — 902 returning to W
904	6.20 am	W	CL	Scoot — shuttle to CL and return to W
905	6.55 am	CL	W	Scoot — 904 returning to W
906	7.08 am	W	CL	Scoot — shuttle to CL and return to W
907	7.40 am	CL	W	Scoot 906 returning to W
908	7.50 am	W	C	Scoot — through to Chicago
909	8.15 am	CL	W	Mine train — work mine
910	8.45 am	W	CL	Mine train returning to CL
911	9.45 am	CL	W	Local freight from CL
912	As required	W	CL	Local freight returning to CL
913	10.18 am	C	W	Scoot — 8.30 from C
914	10.35 am	W	C	Scoot through to Chicago
915	As required	CL	W	Local freight from CL
916	As required	W	CL	Local freight to CL
917	1.18 pm	C	W	Scoot — 11.30 from C
918	1.35 pm	W	C	Scoot — through to Chicago
919	2.00 pm	CL	W	Mine train — work mine
920	2.30 pm	W	CL	Mine train — return to CL
921	3.18 pm	C	W	Scoot — 1.30 from C
922	4.35 pm	W	C	Scoot — through to Chicago
923	As required	CL	W	Local freight from CL
924	As required	W	CL	Local freight to CL
925	6.47 pm	C	W	Scoot — 5.15 from Chicago
926	7.05 pm	W	CL	Scoot — to Chrystal Lake
927	8.10 pm	C	W	Scoot — 6.30 from Chicago
928	8.35 pm	W	C	Scoot — through to Chicago
929	9.15 pm	CL	W	Mine train
930	9.45 pm	W	CL	Mine train — return to CL
931	10.18 pm	CL	W	Scoot — shuttle from CL (926 returning)
932	10.25 pm	W	CL	Scoot — shuttle to CL
933	11.18 pm	CL	W	Scoot (932 returning)
934	11.45 pm	W	CL	Scoot — to CL
901	2.18 am	CL	W	Scoot (934 returning) Lays over at W to form 902

Notes:
C = Chicago, Madison Street Station   W = Warren   CL = Chrystal Lake
All times in column 2 are arrival/departure Warren

than a development from a basic train set oval, has massive operational potential far removed from merely running model trains round and round in circles. When trying to work a full week-day time-table in an evening session there was not actually much time available for running round and round but a few laps to simulate 'mileage' could be put in before bringing a train into the station.

Times are frequently mentioned here, but no real time has been involved, because the schemes suggested are for modellers working in a leisurely way on home layouts. Quite a few people use speeded up clocks to give a real clock and timescale. The main reason for speeding up time for operating purposes is to compensate for lack of distance. A real time-table may allow 1 hour for covering 50 miles, for example, but an express running on a big layout may cover less than a scale ½ mile (800m) in covering the whole layout. Therefore an operator may decide that the five minutes it takes to do this will represent the hour it would have taken in real life. Therefore either five real minutes are taken to depict an hour's

WARREN BERESFORD AND CHICAGO

EFFECTIVE JANUARY 1, 1977

MONDAYS through FRIDAYS

	TO Chicago			FROM Chicago	
Leave Warren	Leave Beresford	Arrive Chicago (See Note)	Leave Chicago (See Note)	Arrive Beresford	Arrive Warren
AM	AM	AM	AM	AM	AM
*5.45	5.55	7.24	*12.30	2.08	2.18
*6.20	6.30	8.00	8.30	10.08	10.18
*7.08	7.18	8.40	11.30	....	....
7.50	8.00	9.28	....	PM	PM
		PM	....	1.08	1.18
10.35	10.45	12.20	....	....	....
1.35	1.45	3.20	1.30	3.08	3.18
4.35	4.45	6.20	•5.15	6.37	6.47
†7.25	7.15	....	....	....	....
8.35	8.45	10.20	6.30	8.00	8.10
†10.25	10.35	....	*8.30	10.08	10.18
†11.45	11.55	....	*9.30	11.08	11.18
PM	AM	PM	AM	PM	AM

SATURDAYS ONLY

	TO Chicago			FROM Chicago	
Leave Warren	Leave Beresford	Arrive Chicago (See Note)	Leave Chicago (See Note)	Arrive Beresford	Arrive Warren
AM	AM	AM	AM	AM	AM
*6.20	6.30	8.05	*12.30	2.08	2.18
*7.00	7.10	8.40	8.30	10.08	10.18
7.50	8.00	9.55			PM
		PM	11.30	1.08	1.18
10.40	10.50	12.25	2.30	4.08	4.18
1.35	1.45	3.20	6.30	8.08	8.18
4.35	4.45	6.20	8.30	10.08	10.18
8.35	8.45	10.20			
PM	PM	PM	AM	AM	AM

SUNDAYS and HOLIDAYS

	TO Chicago			FROM Chicago	
Leave Warren	Leave Beresford	Arrive Chicago (See Note)	Leave Chicago (See Note)	Arrive Beresford	Arrive Warren
AM	AM	AM	AM	AM	AM
7.50	8.00	9.55	*12.30	2.08	2.18
		PM	8.30	10.08	10.18
10.40	10.50	12.25			PM
*12.40	12.50	2.20	10.30	12.08	12.18
4.40	4.50	6.20	2.30	4.08	4.18
6.40	6.50		6.30	8.08	8.18
8.40	8.50	10.20			
PM	PM	PM	AM	AM	AM

AM — LIGHT figures PM — Heavy figures

Note: All trains stop at Clybourn unless otherwise indicated
• — This train does not stop at Clybourn. * — Change trains at Chrystal Lake. † — Service to Chrystal Lake only.

HOLIDAYS

New Year's, Memorial Day, Independence Day, Labor Day, Thanksgiving and Christmas Day

FOR TRAIN INFORMATION

WARREN 546-0758
BERESFORD 546-0758

Or information Chicago 454-6677
6.30 AM to 11.30 PM

CHICAGO AND **NORTH WESTERN** *RAILROAD*
WE'RE EMPLOYEE OWNED

---

running, or an old clock is acquired and altered to run fast so that the passage of one hour on the clock face takes only five minutes real time. The train can then be run to something like a real timetable, complete with the chance of it being late or early as in real life! The five minutes quoted here is an example, incidentally; depending on layout size an 'hour' can take 15 minutes, 10 minutes, or whatever is necessary to depict an hour of real time.

Some American enthusiasts have gone further than this. Because all layouts are of necessity compressed in length and real scale miles are out of the question, even on a big garden layout, it is not possible to depict a route of say, 50 scale miles. But how about 50 'smiles'? The thinking here is to take each foot or yard of track to depict a 'simulated' or 'scale' mile (hence 'smile'), so that 50 miles are depicted by 50 feet of track. Relating a speeded clock to these 'smiles' gives the sort of figures on a timetable which approximate to the real thing.

Generally speaking, however, these ideas are more suited to large layouts where there are several operators because keeping everything running on time calls for dispatchers, yardmasters, station masters, and so on, all responsible for their section of the layout and all in communication with each other down the line as in real life. This stage leads to working out timetable graphs, again as in real life, which plot the path of several trains including connections, and bell codes and other real signal devices, and a modeller aspiring to that will have had plenty of experience in the model railway hobby.

Index